SMALL CAP
MILLIONAIRE

How ordinary people make extrodinary profits trading small cap stocks

BILL ROSS
BHSC, CIM, CFP

FriesenPress

Suite 300 – 990 Fort Street
Victoria, BC, Canada V8V 3K2
www.friesenpress.com

Copyright © 2015 by Bill Ross
First Edition — 2015

All rights reserved.

No part of this publication may be reproduced in any form, or by any means, electronic or mechanical, including photocopying, recording, or any information browsing, storage, or retrieval system, without permission in writing from the publisher.

ISBN
978-1-4602-4297-1 (Hardcover)
978-1-4602-4298-8 (Paperback)
978-1-4602-4299-5 (eBook)

1. Business & Economics, Personal Finance, Investing

Distributed to the trade by The Ingram Book Company

CONTENTS

Disclaimer v

Acknowledgements vii

Introduction ix

Chapter #1
How to position yourself
Before you buy the right small cap stock xiii

Chapter #2
Q2 Thinking and the FABS system 7

Chapter #3
F-Finding the right small cap stocks 31

Chapter #4
Fundamental Analysis of small cap stocks 49

Chapter #5
The Trading Plan 81

Chapter #6
Example Scenarios 97

Chapter #7
My Final Thoughts 115

Bill Ross
Biography: 117

Testimonials 119

Disclaimer

2013 LH OPPORTUNITIES GROUP INC (LHOG)

These publications are protected by Canadian and International copyright laws. All rights reserved. No licence is granted to the user except for the user's personal use only. No part of this publication or its contents may be copied, downloaded, stored in a retrieval system, further transmitted, or otherwise reproduced, stored, disseminated, transferred, or used in any form or by any means, except as permitted by LHOG or smallcapsuccess.com without prior written permission. This publication or its contents are proprietary and are limited to the sole use of LHOG and small cap success.com clients.

Our reports, posts and educational materials are based upon information gathered from a variety of sources believed to be reliable but are not guaranteed as to the accuracy or completeness. The information in any of our postings , reports or educational materials is not intended to be, and shall not constitute, an offer to sell or a solicitation of an offer to buy any security or investment product or service, readers should consult a duly registered financial advisor before making and decision to buy or sell a security. The postings and information in any report or educational material is subject to change without notice, and LHOG assumes no responsibility to update the information in any posting or report. The publisher and or its individual officers, employees, or members of their families might, from time to time, have a position in the securities mentioned and may purchase or sell these securities in the future. The publisher and or its individual officers, employees, or members of their families might from time to time, have financial interest with affiliates of companies whose securities have been discussed by either post or report publication.

Past performance is no guarantee of future results. Inherent in any investment is the potential for loss. This material is being provided for informational purposes only and nothing herein constitutes investment, legal, accounting or tax advice, or a recommendation to buy, sell or hold a security. No recommendation or advice is being given as to whether any investment is suitable for a particular investor. It should not be assumed that any investments in securities, companies, sectors or markets identified and described were or will be profitable.

All information is current as of the date of herein and is subject to change without notice. Any views or opinions expressed may not reflect those of the firm as a whole. Small cap success .com and LHOG does not engage in investment banking, market making or asset management activities of any securities. These returns are from hypothetical portfolios consisting of stocks with small cap success concepts that were rebalanced monthly with zero transaction costs. These are not the returns of actual portfolios of stocks.

Acknowledgements

My wife Sheila
Victor Martinez
The Robert Allen Success academy

Introduction

Give a man a fish feed him for the day, teach a man to fish feed him for a lifetime.
Chinese proverb

The only thing that matters when investing in small cap stocks is a relentless focus on discipline, and portfolio Alpha.

SMALL CAP SUCCESS PORTFOLIO AND PROCESS VERSUS THE TSX SMALL CAP INDEX

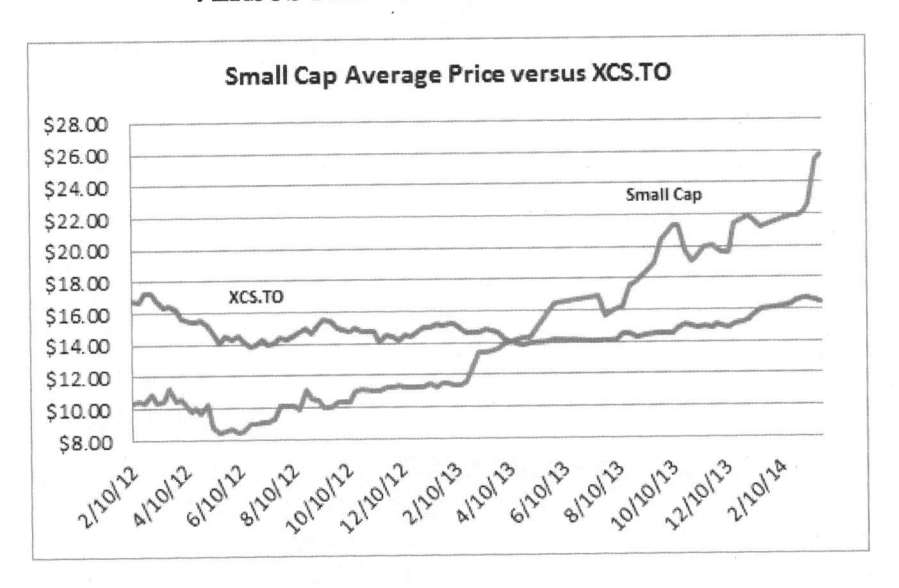

Small Cap Average Price versus XCS.TO

Top Picks 2012-13
Auto Canada (ACQ) 244% ROI
MTY Foods (MTY) 101% ROI
Tourmaline (TOU) 140% ROI

THE WWW.SMALLCAPSUCCESS.COM VALUE PROPOSITION:

Helping train investors to uncover exceptional small cap opportunities, and execute trades with the discipline required to produce exceptional results.

One good trade will pay for an entire year's membership at www.smallcapsuccess.com and set me on the path to financial freedom.

Small cap success Member

When I was at Disneyland with my children for the first time, I remember the attendant taking great care to ensure my two kids were really fastened in well before we headed straight down Magic Mountain.

Investing in small cap stocks can for some people mimic a roller coaster ride. The event can be exhilarating and fun if you understand how and when to get on and off the ride. However if you fail to grasp and follow the basic rules you can put yourself in a very precarious situation. My job is to help you get on and off the small cap ride safely.

"Buckle up" Let's Go.

HOW TRADING SMALL CAP STOCKS CAN CHANGE YOUR LIFE:

How would you feel if you could move from the dog house to the penthouse, never having to work for that obnoxious boss again, achieving financial freedom on your terms?

Imagine finally having the money and time to travel, and best of all financial freedom for the rest of your life to do the things that make you happy and fulfilled. If you're reading this book I assume you're a motivated "self directed investor" looking to build a better life for you and your family .You may also be a professional investor looking to gain some additional Alpha in your clients portfolio's by investing in select small cap issues. Understanding how to pick winning small cap stocks consistently will give you that opportunity.

That's what trading in small cap stocks has done for me, and I would like to share with you some of the winning strategies and tactics I have learned over the past 20 years working as a professional investment manager and entrepreneur in the microcap and small cap space.

As you work through this book you will learn from 2 characters Bob and Sarah. Sarah and Bob will help you walk through my Q2 (Quantitative and Qualitative) thinking process and easy to understand 4 step "FABS" (Find it, analyze it, Buy it, and Sell it) "GARP" (growth at a reasonable price) investment system.

With this system and following some simple trading rules you will have all the tools you will ever need to deliver superior portfolio performance. You will also learn many valuable lessons about what type of an investor you are and how you can maximize your returns, and minimize the mistakes common to most retail investors and even experienced professionals.

SARAH AND BOB, A CONTRAST IN INVESTMENT PHILOSOPHY AND SUCCESS:

Sarah and Bob are partners and have worked together in the same office for over 10 years, S&B engineering Inc. Sarah is 38 years of age, she is a professional engineer and has her mortgage paid off and is well on her way to becoming a millionaire thanks to a solid financial plan and the added returns she and her financial advisor Garth are generating. Her partner Bob is also an engineer 39 years of age but unlike Sarah, Bob is struggling financially.

Sarah and Bob make roughly the same income; however how they manage their money and make investment decisions has led them down very different pathways. Sarah has a well defined Investment plan based on a diversified asset allocation strategy that incorporates a mix of small cap stocks to enhance returns. Sarah and her CFP certified Broker/advisor Garth utilize the small cap success program available at (www.smallcapsuccess.com).

Sarah is fiercely independent she runs both a self directed account and also counts on her advisor Garth to help he make the best decisions she can. Sarah and Garth believe well timed and well researched tactical allocations into small cap stocks can enhance her portfolio return and help her retire sooner.

Bob like many investors has no plan, and believes, tips from friends and lotto tickets are the way to achieve financial freedom. Throughout this book we will look at the decisions Sarah and Bob make in their pursuit to becoming small cap millionaires. We will also examine many of the effective strategies the professional portfolio management community utilizes to drive portfolio returns.

We will help you identify your key behavioral tendencies and blind spots in an effort to avoid the common and not so common mistakes that investors make that negatively impact their returns and lead to anger, frustration and financial regret.

The book will address 6 fundamental areas essential for your success:

1. How to position yourself before you buy a small cap stock

2. Q2 thinking and the FABS small cap trading process

3. Finding the right small cap stock

4. Analyzing small cap stocks

5. The trading plan, buying and selling small cap stocks

6. Practice exercises

Good luck, let's get started

Chapter #1

How to position yourself
Before you buy the right small cap stock

RETURN OF CAPITAL IS AS IMPORTANT AS RETURN ON CAPITAL
WARREN BUFFETT

ASSET ALLOCATION AND PORTFOLIO MANAGEMENT 101:

Discover the importance of asset allocation and portfolio management strategies in your overall investment success.

1. Examine the importance of seeking qualified advice

2. Differentiate the important aspects of managing your money, with an emphasis on long term goals and objective.

3. Discover why you should invest no more than 30% of your total investment portfolio in small cap stocks.

4. Establish why your trading decisions should always be geared around keeping you in the game for the long term.

Before you begin trading small cap stocks it is crucial you have a clear sense of the risk involved in this activity. Trading small cap growth oriented stocks can be a dangerous business if you do not know what you're doing. It can be extremely rewarding if you act correctly or devastating if your analysis leads you in the wrong direction.

Small cap stocks are one of the most volatile asset classes. They tend to be less liquid than other larger cap stocks; less liquidity equals more volatility. In many cases a large number of shares are held by a small number of investors making them susceptible to big trading swings if the news is good or bad. They are notorious for being highly promoted by speculators and are less covered by mainstream analysts making them more vulnerable to manipulation.

For these and a variety of other reasons it is crucial to understand you need to have a solid game plan for your overall portfolio before you engage in trading these instruments. You need to keep your eye on your long term overall portfolio goals and never bite off more risk than you can manage to lose. This is a game of producing solid risk adjusted returns, and creating long term success and financial freedom.

BOB:

Bob makes just over $100,000 per year as an engineer and has over $100,000 in his savings account at the local bank, thanks to an inheritance from his late Uncle Jim; he also has free cash flow of just over $2,000 per month.

Bob thinks he has a great plan; if he invests the $100,000 in 5 small cap stocks that his buddy Al from the bowling team is recommending he could be a millionaire before he knows it. He will spend the rest of the money on holidays and a new Dodge Charger.

You see, his buddy Al from the bowling team made some money last year off a tip from his friend Stan who got the tip from his friend Jason. Jason's brother Steve worked for a small oil and Gas Company and the company hit it big in the Bakken oil fields of North Dakota.

Al has just received another tip from another friend who says he has the next big thing in the food industry. Bioexx (BXI) is listed on the Toronto exchange and looks great, says Al; returns could be 10 times your money. Bob agrees to take a look and after being all pumped up on news releases and conference calls by the CEO, decides to invest all $100,000 at $2.35.

Bob can't wait to become a millionaire.

SARAH:

Sarah on the other hand, who acts as her own personal chief executive officer (CEO) when it comes to her investments, visits her long-time financial advisor Garth.

Garth is a certified financial planner and (CFP) acts as her Chief financial officer (CFO) ,continuously monitors and revisits her total wealth and retirement plan quarterly. Sarah tells Garth she has just received a recent raise at work and has also come into $100,000 from an unexpected inheritance. She wants to keep the inheritance money safe for retirement in a well diversified portfolio and is looking to put more of her monthly income towards the small cap portfolio, approximately $2,000 per month.

Garth who holds both investment manager and financial planning designations advises her to allocate 100% of her inherited funds into the existing well designed and diversified retirement portfolio which they had set up a number of years ago. That portfolio was developed in accordance with her long term objectives and risk tolerance in mind.

Based on Sarah's risk tolerance and long term objectives Garth's suggested a balanced allocation which has a dividend income tilt. The portfolio includes, 5-10% cash, 40% diversified fixed income, 40% equities (including preferred shares), 10% extended asset classes such as high quality REITs', Gold and other precious metals, mature yield oriented private equity, and market neutral hedge funds. The portfolio is further diversified by geography, market cap, sector, and manager style. Her target long term return for the retirement account is 7% with a moderate to low risk profile.

The remaining $2000 cash flow will be allocated to a separate account with a very different mandate. The focus will be growth and will focus on higher risk higher return small and micro cap issuers. The funds will initially be placed in money market account where it can be accessed for investing in the small cap stocks they pick together using the small cap success program and strategies.

Garth's oversight ensures no more than 30% of her overall portfolio be allocated to these high quality smaller issuers. He will rebalance both portfolios annually to ensure the investment policy statement meets all the suggested target allocation ranges.

BOB:

The quarterly and annual review.

Bob is a pure do it yourself guy which is fine as long as you still follow an appropriate asset allocation and systematic trading approach based on your long term financial objectives and clearly identified risk tolerance parameters . Self-directed investors willing to spend the time can save a material amount in advisory fees, however the results have to match expectations. I have always found being an engaged investor and working with an advisor is the best approach because you take the best ideas from both camps and work towards a collective outcome; it's the end game results that matter.

Bob was not happy with his year end results. After a series of bad news releases over the course of the year, Bioexx closes at 1.0 cent. Bob did not have any trading plan or stop loss strategies to minimize the impact; he rode the stock down to zero thinking to the last minute it was poised for a rebound. Bob suffered from over confidence, regret aversion and failure to act.

These are common behavioral finance traits found in the unsophisticated and untrained investor. Bob failed to ruthlessly sell his negative position and never had another winning stock in his portfolio to offset the Bioexx loss. To that end Bob paid a heavy price.

At the bowling alley Al apologizes to Bob; no one saw that coming, not even the sell side analysts from the corporate finance group promoting the stock to their clients.

Have no fear says Bob. My aunt Helen is very ill and I am expecting another $250,000. I won't make that mistake again.

SARAH:

Sarah's diversified portfolio is up 6.5% net of fees, and with very low volatility Sarah is sleeping well at night. She and Garth have also picked 5 winning trades out of 10 using Q2 thinking and the www.smallcapsuccess.com "FABS" approach; her return on the small cap portfolio is 17.5%. She has let the winners run and ruthlessly sold off any stocks that have declined as per protocol allowing Garth to also sleep well. Garth and here have rebalanced the portfolio to ensure compliance with the overall stated investment policy allocation and Sarah remains well on her way to becoming a millionaire.

BOB:

Bob is still waiting and will likely repeat the losing process over if he ever gets the chance. Bob has essentially taken himself out of the game by not looking at his total portfolio and long term goals. Bob had materially over relied on 1 stock to deliver and did not recognize his key behavioral tendencies and blind spots that would ultimately destroy his wealth.

APPLYING THE LESSONS LEARNED:

- Seek good advice
- Diversify with your long term goals in mind
- Understand your behavioral blind spots and stay in the game
- Ruthlessly sell the losers and ride the winners
- Continuously evaluate and rebalance your portfolio
- Keep it simple; complexity does not always work in your favour

CASE REVIEW:

You have saved some money over the past 10 years ($100,000) and are looking at investing some of that money in small cap stocks. You have elected to put $10,000 of the $100,000 into a small cap portfolio.

What should you do next?

    a. Invest all $10,000 into 1 stock recommended by my friend.

    b. Talk to an unqualified advisor and invest $100,000 into the small cap portfolio as per his firms' recommendation. They are promoting a new issue he says is guaranteed to be a winner. He asks you to write him a cheque made out to him personally and he will put it into your investment account.

    c. Go see Garth and first determine if the $10,000 allocation to small caps was appropriate. Assume it was determined that $10,000 was the correct allocation size based on the long term goals and risk tolerance. I would invest the $10,000 into a diversified small cap portfolio using exchange traded funds or mutual funds and may place some of the funds in individual stocks selected utilizing the small cap success program.

    d. Place all $10,000 into 10-20 small cap stocks utilizing a self-directed account and finding those trading ideas and strategies utilizing the small cap success program.

    e. C or D

Correct Answer: E

I personally believe C would be the best approach, however if you are a self-directed investor and are confident in your process and committed to trading individual small cap stocks then D would also be an appropriate higher risk approach.

Chapter #2

Q2 Thinking and the FABS system

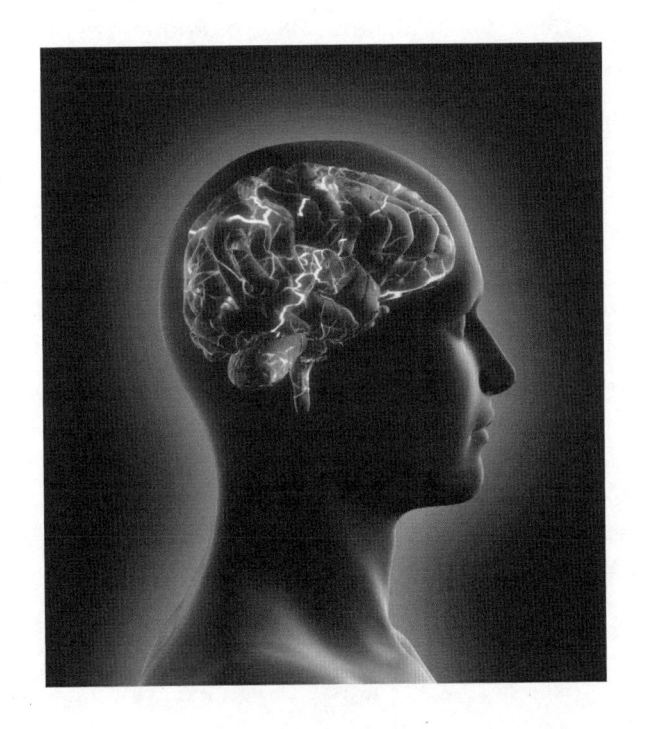

INVESTING IS SIMPLE BUT NOT EASY
WARREN BUFFETT

LEARNING OUTCOME:

Evaluating and identifying key attributes and processes needed to become a successful small cap investor.

1. How to effectively apply both (Q2)qualitative and quantitative strategies when investing

2. Discover why Q2 thinking really matters

3. Distinguishing your behavioral blind spots

4. Formulate why you need a systematic process to select small cap stocks

5. Identify and evaluate the key elements of the 4 step FABS process

Warren Buffet, arguably the world's most successful investor and the heart of the Berkshire Hathaway success story, has said investing is simple but not easy. I can attest to that, after 20 years of investing both as an amateur and professional in the investment industry, I have certainly had some great wins but also more than my share of disappointments.

For the most part investing is not rocket science although some areas of the discipline can be more complex than others. For most amateur and even professional investors having a simple repeatable investment philosophy and approach is imperative. Building the investment trading platform is simple; the tough part is having the discipline to execute objectively and unemotionally is where things can and usually do fall apart.

Money ball was a phrase coined by the baseball industry as a result of the amazing success of the Oakland A's in the 1980's; the movie was a big hit with Brad Pitt playing the lead role. The Oakland A's built a winning franchise in the 1980's and did so at a fraction of the cost as compared to the New York Yankees or the Boston Red Sox, a truly remarkable achievement.

The driver for their success was that Oakland management had moved from a purely subjective player assessment approach to a much more structured quantitative statistical assessment and a secondary qualitative view of each member of their squad; Q2 Thinking (Quantitative and Qualitative).

What the Oakland management had discovered is that baseball games were won and lost by getting more batters on base more often which led to more runs and untimely more wins. In essence they began utilizing statistical and qualitative analysis methods on each player to change the probabilities of success on the field.

Money ball – Q2 thinking for the small cap trader is in my view a more effective approach to achieving your life's dreams than the more common, hit and hope strategy that most follow. Discipline and utilizing a time tested approach will get you to where you want to be and you will do so with much less risk of financial ruin.

Money ball, for the small cap **Growth at A Reasonable Price** (GARP) trader is the Q2 "FABS" system and it all starts with Q2 thinking.

Q2 THINKING

When trading small cap stocks, understanding how to select the right stocks and ultimately selling them in a timely fashion are key drivers to your success. Q2 Thinking involves 2 fundamental processes, quantitative and qualitative screening to select what we believe to be the superior opportunities. More importantly it involves a quantitative and qualitative view as to when to sell, avoiding dangerous behavioral biases.

Your left brain and right brain must work in concert with specifically designed processes and tools to achieve Q2 equilibrium and the strongest performance results. It is imperative that you strike the right balance between simply crunching the raw data (quantitative modelling) and using your gut instincts to make decisions (qualitative modelling).

There are many platforms and asset management firms that are moving to pure quantitative models with great success, however for the most part the majority of the firms we work with use this hybrid Q2 approach.

BEHAVIORAL FINANCE 101: THE EMOTIONAL SIDE OF INVESTING

Money is not just a commodity used for executing transactions, it is bundled emotion. How you manage those emotions is one of the key differentiators in determining your success or failure.

A long dissertation on behavioral finance is beyond the scope of this book; however having some awareness of how you may act when it comes to the emotions associated with managing money may be helpful in the understanding and improvement of your trading patterns and actions. It will defiantly help you with both aspects of your Q2 thinking.

Creating the quantitative screens and reviewing the data is the easy part. The more challenging aspect of investing for me has always been the emotional side. In fact the reason I developed this program and trading rules was to decrease my behavioral tendencies (blind spots) that would get me into trouble.

NEVER FORGET "YOU ARE YOUR OWN WORST ENEMY"

I believe each investor comes with a hard wired blueprint of how they will anchor themselves to a stock position; some manager's operate under strict rules and try to keep the emotional demons at bay. Many asset managers take pride in the ability to navigate both sides of this sharp knife.

The key is to understand how you are hard wired, what those individual tendencies are that will manifest under pressure and trip you up. Most importantly it is the understanding of the strategies that will keep you out of trouble when executing trades.

HARD WIRING: NEURO-ECONOMICS AND TAMING THE DEMONS

You cannot maximize your wealth if you cannot master your mind and emotions. The science of neuro-economics takes a look at how your mind works as it relates to money and finance.

Neuro-economics is a hybrid science, looking at neuroscience, economics and psychology in an effort to understand what drives our collective investing decisions. It is a relatively new science and there is still much to learn but researchers have identified a number of key elements all investors should be aware of.

You have likely heard the expression, buy low and sell high, yet most buy high and sell low. You have heard work hard, study intensely and more data will give you an edge, but in many ways it seems to just confuse you and lead to more mistakes.

Most investors do the opposite to the logical, principally because of two emotions, fear and greed. When you're scared your body hits the flight and fight response and you hit the sell button at exactly the wrong time. When you're feeling on top of the world because you're so much smarter than everyone else you hit the greed button and double down by buying stocks using leverage at ridiculous valuations.

We would like to think our brain operates perfectly all the time but the reality is it does not, so you have to have systems and processes to tame the emotion demons when they take hold of you.

Knowing who you are is critical and it usually comes with making many mistakes and losing money. A friend of mine calls it the tuition; unfortunately this can be very expensive education if you do not learn very quickly.

NEURO-ECONOMIC BASICS:

Your mind has 3 basic processing areas that get triggered when trading.

Greed –Anticipation of a potential win= produces a biochemical High

Crystallization-Realization of profit or loss = produces a biochemical Low or depression

Fear of a potential loss= produces a strong adrenalin response, fight or flight

Stock market Wins:

- Making money or losing money on a trade is not merely a physical gain or loss on your account statement but an emotional win or loss you put in the memory banks.

- The anticipation of making money brings you the same neurological biochemical response –BUZZ as ingesting cocaine or other mind altering stimulants. After repeated wins your body gets to like the response and it can be rather intoxicating to even think about a huge win.

- However it should be noted even when you realize on a win it can seem rather anti- climactic and disappointing and may produce a biochemical low.

LOSSES:

- Fear of losing money can trigger a serious flight and fight response; you panic and make all the wrong moves at the worst time. Selling when everyone else is selling is common (herd behavior). This is especially difficult to resist today when all the quantitative trading platforms hit the auto sell button and the market goes into full panic mode. By fighting the fear and understanding market behavior I have found many great opportunities to buy high value stocks during an abnormal market sell-offs, only to then sell them right back into the market once the panic abates. It should be noted that the fear factor emotional response can be 2 times as powerful as the greed factor.

- Fear can and will drive you crazy and ultimately destroy your portfolio returns if you let it. Our goal is to help investors understand that fear is normal and can be managed with strict trading rules and discipline.

COMMON EMOTIONAL AND COGNITIVE BEHAVIORAL TENDENCIES TO BE AWARE OF:

First and foremost the financial services industry is well aware of these tendencies and plays to them, so be very aware when you see unscrupulous brokers and investor relations folks attempting to solicit certain responses from you. Emotional biases are typically driven by the desire to avoid loss or unadulterated greed.

Cognitive biases are usually the result of investors looking for shortcuts and fast money. They are most attracted to unproven decision making processes and lack substantive information to make logical decisions. Every investor has elements of all of these biases, but you will likely lean towards 1-2 forms, which if not managed appropriately under pressure can destroy you financially and personally.

I have seen it first hand with a company called Bioexx Specialty Proteins Ltd (BXI) on the Toronto Stock Exchange (TSX). Check out the old blogs on stockhouse.com. If they are still there you will get an eye opener on the damage caused when things go terribly wrong.

One fellow who was a regular blogger put his whole life savings into the stock, and then even doubled down by leveraging the equity in his house, rolling it all into a stock that went to zero on him. His behavioral bias' ultimately destroyed his marriage and left him homeless. Now that's powerful!

BEHAVIORAL BIASES:

- **Regret Aversion - Emotional Bias**: sometimes you fail to make any decisions because you have a fear of regret. This happens especially if you have lost money on a trade; the larger the loss the more regret. It is a primary reason we spend a lot of time on the trading plan and expectations.

- **Illusion of Control- Emotional**: The false belief that you're in control. Guaranteed when it comes to anything to do with the markets you're not in control. Just when you think you are you will find yourself more out of control than ever. Even the dealers who sit at the top of the investment food chain can and often do find themselves facing unpredictable Black Swan events. The markets are unpredictable; accept that you have no control over future events and learn to adapt quickly, or perish.

- **Overconfidence-Cognitive bias**: Excessive confidence in one's ability to predict and make decisions. Thinking, you are so much smarter of have better information then the market. This is a common trait among the more highly educated or better connected investor. A good rule I discuss in our webcasts is the "market is always right" rule; basically when the tape moves against you, it does not matter how smart you think you are. The bottom line is the market is yelling at you to move, and you have to cut your loss and move on to the next winning idea or be prepared to lose your capital. I know from experience that this is a key hot button for me personally.

- **Over Optimism-Emotional Bias**: It's good to be positive but over optimism can cloud your judgement. Being over sold a hot story is a key trigger point for a good salesman/stock broker. If there is too much optimism in a stock and you are over excited, be careful.

- **Loss Aversion-Emotional bias:** Avoiding choices that may result in the crystallization of a loss. This is by far one of the challenging aspects of investing. No one likes to lose money and admitting you were wrong is painful, but imperative to your success. Cutting losers quickly is an essential element in the trading and money management process.

- **Cognitive Dissonance-Cognitive**: Rationalizing your decisions to avoid change and acceptance. "I won't sell even though I am down 50%, because next week things will be better when the weather changes and the company releases those new drilling numbers I have been waiting for."

- **Self-Attribution-Cognitive**: Attributing your wins to skill and your losses to the randomness of the markets.

- **Confirmation- Cognitive:** Focusing your attention on news that reinforces your view. This is a huge danger. Always carry a high degree of skepticism about your ideas, seek out contrary news, opinions; I think of it as the "prove me wrong" approach.

- **Hindsight-Cognitive:** Exaggerated memory of one's conviction about past decisions. Looking back you have unrealistic memories of what and how you reacted. This is why I recommend you take notes on every trade, as these reflections will reinforce your learnings and make you a better trader.

- **Endowment-Emotional:** You have researched the story and have owned the stock for some time; you love the management and the idea behind the stock and it's hard to let go even in the face of obvious selling by the market. Endowment bias is favoritism toward a stock based on your feelings of ownership. Never fall in love with a stock or story; it will always break your heart if you do.

- **Status Quo- Emotional:** You do not like change. If that's you go buy a GIC as there is no room for you in small cap stocks or anywhere near the markets.

- **Anchoring and Adjustment-Cognitive**: Stubbornly hanging on to old forecasts, predictions and news. In the face of new information you must act or be slaughtered by those that do. Failure to get out of a burning house means you will likely die.

- **Representativeness-Cognitive:** Allowing past experiences to shape your interpretation of new information and future decisions.

- **Availability-Cognitive**: Favoring easily accessed information over full information. Looking at media driven reports and news stories on the net versus fundamental due diligence.

- **Conservatism-Cognitive**: Failure to recognize that the new information has value. This can be a challenging one, and comes with experience. After a while you get very good at looking at what is meaningful and relevant. It is key to any success in the markets.

- **Recency-Cognitive**: Looking at recent information from a historical bias. A good example would be looking at recent positive drilling results for a junior oil and gas company, with a view that the results cannot be all that good because the management team has never gotten it right before.

- **Ambiguity aversion-Cognitive**: Avoiding risk during periods of uncertainty. This may be a blessing at times but as always moderation of one's bias is the key. If you never take a chance you can never expect a reward. Playing the markets successfully is all about calculated risk taking.

- **Framing-Cognitive:** Varying a decision process based on your personal view or chosen context. Some investors have a certain view of things and can make money; quite often taking a contrarian view can open your eyes up to a world of other possibilities. If you only have 1 frame of reference you can miss the bigger picture.

With a list like that facing your every decision how will you ever function trading small cap stocks?

SIMPLE STRATEGIES TO KEEP YOU OUT OF TROUBLE:

"Focus on a specific habitat you know well, do fundamentally sound due diligence, stick to your discipline, monitor and review your decisions and portfolio regularly".
Have a plan and set realistic goals for trading

Revaluate every trade and note any behavioral tendencies, especially when you lose.

- Be patient

- Avoid market noise, stick to your process

- Manage the portfolio and the size of your positions correctly, stay in the game

- Stick to higher quality issuers, they offer you better protection in volatile markets

- When you make a mistake, learn from it and move on

- Understand the market has a million moving parts and you have no control over it, so manage your process and expectations accordingly.

- Trust your gut but verify your decisions

A COUPLE GOOD BOOKS ON THE SUBJECT:

Your money your brain by, Jason Zweig

The little book of behavioral investing, James Montier

Blink, Malcolm Gladwell

THE FABS PROCESS OVERVIEW:
FIND IT, ANALYZE IT, BUY IT, AND SELL IT.

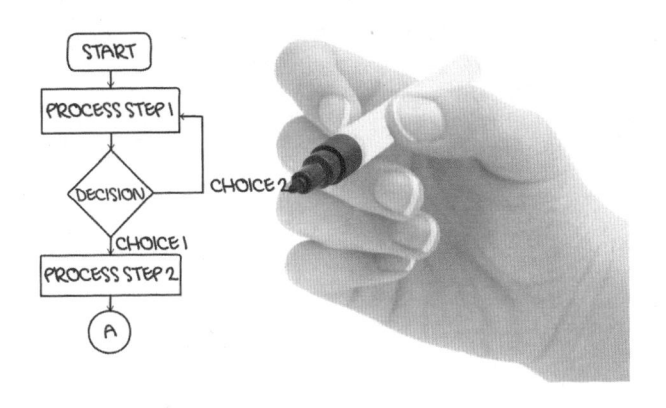

FABS- MAKING THE INVESTING PROCESS A LITTLE EASIER

Having a well-defined investment philosophy and trading process will hopefully save you from yourself. Working hard and executing with discipline will help you produce the results you want. Before we walk you through the actual steps it is important to understand the rational for the individual elements and how they work together to produce the desired result.

The easy to use and highly effective 4 step **"FABS"** process is designed to repeatedly hit a series of singles, doubles and the occasional bases loaded home run, to use the baseball analogy. This game is all about staying diversified with a high percentage of your retirement money and maximizing your return potential with small cap stocks.

Minimizing the risk of losing your money and executing the process as cheaply as possible is a key objective. Positive Risk adjusted returns net of fees and taxes creates wealth, and that is what you're looking for. Tax mitigation is also part of an effective trading and wealth creation strategy and we will touch on that topic briefly, however a comprehensive view of that topic is beyond the scope of this book. This platform is about creating wealth over time, and trading small cap stocks can do that for you, but you have to understand the game and execute with precision

Q2 THINKING AND TRADING SKILLS:

He who learns but does not think, is lost!
He who thinks but does not learn is in great danger.
Confucius

Like any great athlete, it takes time energy and effort to master a skill and achieve great success. In the book *Outliers*, Malcolm Gladwell talks about the notion of 10,000 hours to mastery. He studied the ultra-successful outliers and a common trait was early skill development and persistence.

If you're reading this book you have the desire to make a fortune trading small-cap stocks. What you need now are the tools and the time to master the skills. My hope is that this endeavour will not take you the same 10,000+ hours it took me to learn how to swim with the sharks and not get eaten.

Trading small-cap stocks is one of the fastest ways to make a fortune and become financially independent to do the things you've always dreamed of. It is also the fastest ways to lose money if you do not follow the rules of the road.

Think of small cap trading like driving a Ferrari, if you do it well the experience can be exhilarating and fun; do it poorly and recklessly, well you know what can happen.

Small cap trading is a vehicle that you can use to make all those dreams come true. You know you have the motivation and a strong desire to succeed and are willing to put in the work, but you are likely asking yourself if you have all the required tools and skills to succeed.

Our job is to help you identify any gaps and fill them with the right skills, knowledge and ability to execute, producing the fastest results without crashing and burning.

After 20 years of trading stocks both as an amateur and professional I believe the 4 step FABS process is one of the most efficient ways to accomplish your goals. Before we move forward with each of the elements of the FABS process lets first examine why we tend to look predominantly at small cap GARP stocks and stick to a particular habitat.

WHAT IS GARP AND WHY DO WE INVEST IN GARP STOCKS? WHAT DOES A SMALL CAP GARP STOCK LOOK LIKE?

Firstly we should recognize that investing in small cap growth stories is inherently more risky than say investing in large cap dividend paying value stories. Given that I think it is fair to say that we should do what we can to minimize our risk where we can. Purchasing over hyped and overvalued small cap stocks to me is inherently more risky than finding good undervalued small cap growth opportunities that have a demonstrated earnings profile.

If you break the term GARP down in to its essential elements what we're looking at is a stock with a growth profile trading at a reasonable price relative to its perceived intrinsic value

(Growth at a reasonable price)

Intrinsic value is a fancy way of estimating what a stock should be worth based on its current earnings per share picture and a future growth profile; or its ability to generate wealth for its shareholders.

Benjamin Graham, Warren Buffett's mentor is considered the god father of securities analysis. He suggests the intrinsic value (IV) can be determined by:

IV= EPS X (8.5 + (2X forecast annual earnings)

He later revised the formula to account for the fact that valuations can vary depending on interest rate fluctuations.

His revised formula:

IV=EPS X (4.4/AAA bond X (8.5 + (2 X forecast annual earnings growth rate)

For example:

If you had a company with $1.00 per share earnings, and the bond yield was 5.2% with a forecast earnings growth of 20% the stock price should arguably be:1.0X4.4/5.2 X (8.5 + (2 X20) = $41.03

If the stock was trading below that number it would be considered trading below its intrinsic value and a good candidate to look at.

Most amateur small cap growth investors do not spend much time grinding through complex valuation methodologies. The reason is that there are just too many variables that can change the earnings projections with these immature growth stories. However recognizing the basic elements of how valuation is viewed and created is important to all investors. If the pros recognize and make decisions based on valuation metrics you have to recognize that it is a key element in what drives the market, and you need to recognize the key drivers of stock moves.

WHY WE LIKE SMALL CAP GARP STOCKS: GROWTH AT A REASONABLE PRICE

Most investors look for a balance between price and the expected growth in earnings going forward. In essence they want to buy growth at a reasonable price (GARP). This is determined by looking at the stock's price to earnings ratio (PE) and its expected growth rate (THE PEG ratio)

PEG= PE/forecast EPS growth.
A PEG at 1.0 indicates fair value
Below 1.0 indicates undervalued
Above 1.0 indicates over valued

During bullish times the growth investor may raise the fair value PEG ratio to 2.0 to reflect the bullishness in the street. The bottom line here is that the only thing we really know for a fact is the price, which is the last closing price; all the other factors are open to the currents of unpredictable future events. Nonetheless it gives you a feel for valuation and whether a stock is overvalued or the rates used in the assumptions are appropriate.

My feelings are that a PEG ratio can be helpful but it is only 1 metric in a series of metrics we look at. But if you are consistently over paying for hyped up and pumped up small cap dreams, you are going to lose money. Adding some valuation metrics into the process can help you filter many losers out of the mix before they ever get in and erode your capital.

FABS:

The FABS process will incorporate both quantitative and qualitative skills (Q2 thinking).

The first step in the process is F- finding what we believe may be some of the best opportunities in the small-cap space and our preferred habitat. We use what we call the small-cap growth analysis quick Tier-1 technical screen and will walk you through step by step how this process works.

Step number two is A-analyzing the stocks we have found and determining what we think are the best movers and long term opportunities. We will be looking at both the key fundamental and technical variables that you need to know in hopes of avoiding egregious missteps, landmines and financial cockroaches that are occasionally lying hidden underneath the story.

It is the unknown that all too often catches you and destroys your wealth. We follow the cockroach theory, which is to suggest there is never just one cockroach lurking. When you see one there's probably more and you have to get out immediately avoiding further destruction.

A FINANCIAL COCKROACH IS A SURPRISE MATERIAL NEGATIVE EVENT: EG

- *CEO or CFO lying*
- *Falsifying financial statements*
- *Regulatory infractions by insiders*

The third step in the process is B- Buying; what decisions you make before you commit to buying a stock. How is the stock trading technically? Do the fundamentals all line up? Who is in on the institutional side? What about the insiders: how much do they own, and have they been buyers or sellers?

Other key questions:

- What is the valuation?
- Am I buying at a reasonable price or could I be overpaying?
- Am I buying the best of the best opportunities that are trading undervalued or those that have great momentum metrics that you think are going to continue to move the stock forward? Buying at the right time and at the right price is a very important part of the process.

The last area, but certainly not the least, is the S-Sell step. I think one of the most important if not the most important aspect of any trading process or system in the small cap space is when to sell and take profits or cut a loss. Selling is the key element that separates winners from losers. Utilizing both technical and fundamental analysis in your decision-making process is crucial.

So there you have it, the four key elements that will drive your success. If you execute them with diligence, care, consistency and passion you're going to have great success. In the next few chapters we will walk you through step by step each of the key elements and give you an opportunity to practice some of these moves before you go live yourself.

MY DEMONS

I've been in the investment business as a professional advisor for over 15 years and have traded money for many of Calgary's finest high net worth clients. I have also traded in my own accounts for over 20+ years. Over that time I learned a few things that really matter about driving investment success.

I've lived through the full gamut of emotions both with my own capital and with my client's money. Learning to manage my own emotions and stay in the now was a key factor in my success. Putting these strategies together over time and developing an appreciation and understanding of the things that drive my own behavioral biases and trading decisions has certainly made me a more efficient investor.

Until you've experienced the ups and downs of the market it's really difficult to develop the right attitude and discipline to become a successful investor. What I found over the years is the discipline and a willingness to continue to learn are probably the most important things you can do to enhance your returns.

When I was 18 years old I made my first trade in a junior mining stock. I can't remember its name but I do remember the feeling that I got when that tip from a friend paid off. I had bought the stock for somewhere just under 20 cents and ultimately sold the stock for just over a dollar. I remember thinking to myself as a young man this is an absolutely amazing way to make money. The anticipation of mega returns was intoxicating; I was already spending the money in my mind before the tape had even moved. This was certainly better than grinding away at my regular job. I had a landscaping business when I was 18 and it could be a significant amount of work at times without much financial reward in relative terms.

I had put in about $3,000 at the time, had an amazing return and life was good. I really started to understand the value of the ability to create income passively through the stock market. There is no other system on the planet that allows you to create more money faster and deliver the opportunity of financial success. Fortunately or unfortunately, I had no clue the trade was pure luck and that the win would shape my future losses.

I played around in the market a bit more over the following couple of years, and after saving more money I began buying some mutual funds and trying a variety of other investment vehicles, learning as much as I could while still working at my regular job.

By now I was working with the fire department as a firefighter paramedic but still carried a passion for investing and business. I learned an awful lot about the stock market and business, taking business and securities training courses at the same time as trading my own account. I had some solid wins but quite frankly I had more losses, and a few which were big!. that the experience still resonates with me today. I call it the "tuition" and all investors go through this at some time until they develop discipline and a process.

I bought a stock called Carmanah Resources, not based on a system that I had developed but based on a tip from a friend of mine. The friend, who is still close to me and my family today by the way, was an industry professional and had what we both thought was superior knowledge about the stock at that time. He was a new analyst with a brokerage firm called James Capel.

SMALL CAP MILLIONAIRE

The company in question (Carmanah) was a junior oil and gas opportunity with a big seismic anomaly off the coast of Indonesia. The recommendation from the firm was a speculative buy and the recommendation from my friend was a strong buy. You can probably see the disconnect. At the time, I did not; all I saw was dollars, and lots of them if the well they were about to drill was successful.

I think at the time the stock was trading at $1.65, but estimates were $60.00 if we struck black gold! They had laid out a drill program on a field they called Natuna, a potentially large reservoir. My friend being close to the story had explained the geology and had numerous conversations with the Chief Executive Officer and felt strongly that this could be a real winner.

So I had invested $30,000 in the stock, most of my hard earned portfolio at the time at around $1.65. Over the next 8 weeks while they were preparing the well for drilling the stock had moved to $9.00. If I had made that trade today I would certainly have stripped off a significant amount of those profits, understanding now that even under a best case scenario that well likely only had a 20% chance of success. This was complex geology and 3D seismic imaging was none existent at the time.

However being an amateur and being greedy at the time, I had felt that if the stock hit, it would likely trade north of $50 and make me very wealthy. I failed to see the downside of my decision and behavioral bias.

I let it all ride. The drilling that was planned for Friday afternoon did not go as planned. By late Friday we had a bit of an inclination that something was wrong and that we may not be in a good place Monday at the market open.

Information moves fast in the oil and gas industry in spite of all the rules around timely disclosure. We had some early indications from the street that there was some gas in the wellbore but no oil. Everyone went radio silent on us and, it did not look good. Sure enough by Saturday morning the word was out on Natuna. The stock was halted Monday morning and when it had opened it had fallen by over 50%. By the time it closed for the day it had gone from nine dollars to just over four dollars.

At the open the next day I asked my buddy what he thought and if I should sell. As a novice investor you would think it would be an easy decision, down 50% in 1 day but still ahead overall. The answer was no. I held on thinking it would recover back to $5.00 based on some other projects it had in the pipeline, and then I would sell. Unfortunately Institutional support for Carmanah Resources disintegrated quickly along with the share price. Only a few short weeks later this stock ultimately ended up at zero when it went no-bid and Carmanah Resources closed their doors shortly after that.

Within a 4 to 6 week timeframe the episode went from largely optimistic to a fiery death along with my portfolio. Not only did I lose my original capital of $30,000 but the profits as well. Those demons, greed and fear had paralyzed and beaten me down on this occasion. I had made many foolish decisions but learned a few valuable lessons along the way.

Evaluate the options independently of external influences and act based on your assumptions, not the advice of others. My gut instinct was correct but I failed to act. Do not rely on others or blame others for the decisions made, learn and move on. Another important lesson I learned from this trade was:

Emotions and investor psychology drives the stock market and I learned that lesson all too well myself. The bottom line is there has to be a systematic and proven method to your trading if you want to create superior returns over time. If you're following a time tested system you can win.

I've learned over the years watching some of the best in the business how they make their money. How they consistently outperform the market and where their returns come from. Most importantly I have learned how the capital markets really work, especially in the small-cap space and to respect and manage myself efficiently given where I sit in the investment industry food chain.

My goal as I have said is to share with you in the book what I've learned over 20 years as an amateur and professional trader. Hopefully you can learn from my errors and pay a smaller tuition than I did. That being said there is no magic bullet here and no single way to do this. There is no guarantee on every trade and anybody who suggests that there is either very lucky (unlikely) or is not telling the truth.

Winning in the stock market takes time, energy, effort and above all else, discipline. You have to learn discipline and study the best in the business; learn from them and be patient with yourself as you make your mistakes.

I look at asset managers like Dennis Gartman, Alan Jacobs, Warren Buffet, Peter Lynch, Bill Gross, Sir John Templeton, George Soros and Kiril Sokoloff and try to take the best ideas and mold them into what works for me.

What I've done in developing the FABS process is taken what I believe are the key metrics and strategies you can utilize to drive portfolio performance.

- Beware of your behavioral biases and act appropriately
- Be patient, investing is simple but not easy
- Follow a disciplined process like FABS
- Become a lifelong learner
- Do not overpay for stocks and invest in the habitat you know
- Ruthlessly sell losers, let the winners run, and taking profit is never a bad idea.
- Act independently and never blame others for your decisions

Sarah and Bob have been chatting with friends about which stocks make the most sense given all the volatility in the market. You are looking to them and others to help you make great go forward decisions relative to your investment decisions. The best approach would be:

    a. Bob suggests reading the newspaper and watching TV. He says taking the ideas right off the front page or from well-known TV commentators is the best way to go.

    b. Sarah works with her advisor Garth to generate ideas. They use a variety of sources and tools to make selections. The ideas are based on their own independent analysis and confirmed with multiple sources.

    c. A friend suggests you talk with a fellow named Bernie Madoff; he has heard he is pretty good. Unfortunately, Bernie is tied up right now serving 100 years for committing financial fraud on his clients.

    d. You could utilize the smallcapsuccess.com program and consider private coaching sessions to enhance your skills and ability as it relates to developing a systematic process and a clear understanding of your behavioral biases.

    e. B and E

Correct answer: E

My first choice would be B, working with a good advisor. However, depending on your investment style and objectives you may look to work more independently. The key is to have a process and understand the key drivers to your success.

Chapter #3

F-Finding the right small cap stocks

THE TIER 1 QUICK SCREEN

I'M A GREATER BELIEVER IN LUCK, AND I FIND THE HARDER I WORK THE MORE I HAVE OF IT
THOMAS JEFFERSON

LEARNING OUTCOME:

Discover and apply key selection criteria to your stock selection process

LEARNING OBJECTIVES:

1. Choose the best investments for a select group of small cap stocks

2. Examine the impact of an automatic selection process in picking small cap stocks

3. Develop strategies and tactics to identify key Tier 1 stock selection filters

4. Compare and contrast different investment habitats and their significance in picking top Tier small cap stocks

5. Apply key Tier 1 metrics to your selection process

THE TIER 1 QUICK SCREEN FILTERING PROCESS:

Not unlike launching a new product or service, filtering out the bad ideas and finding the gems that produce strong economic results is what drives business success. Filtering is also one of the major steps that drive investing success.

Initially finding what we believe to be the best opportunity stocks is what we call filtering. It is the initial screen that primarily separates good opportunities from bad ones. Small-cap stocks tend to be under covered by research analysts and good opportunities can remain overlooked, illiquid and sometimes infrequently traded.

Institutional fund managers also have investment mandates that limit the ability to own certain small cap stocks. Until those stocks hit certain thresholds for market cap, weekly volume and price they may go unrecognized by the main stream investment community. Because of this we have literally thousands of stocks to look at and choose from, that present great growth opportunities.

Determining which opportunities are the best is the key, and one of the things that we've learned over the years is how to filter efficiently and effectively and buy stocks that have finally hit the institutional investment eye.

Typical stock selection involves taking a name you have heard through industry traffic or is reported to you by some sell side research analyst or promoter who carries the stock in their research universe. They issue an initiation report followed up by quarterly updates. The buy side analyst, broker or portfolio manager would then break down the sell side research and determine using analytic models to see if the story makes sense. In some shops they may even restrict their internal brokers to their own internal research or a few select sources they control; this lack of independent thought is a huge problem in the industry and leads to client firm conflict of interests.

It's not uncommon for a firm's corporate finance group working a new issue to put the pressure on the research group. Research issues a glowing report, they send the report out to the broker community and there you have fully unbiased research; well, not quite. As a manger you do your best to analyze all the facts you can before making recommendations to clients but your idea generation universe gets pretty small if you do not have a wide net and choices of names to choose from.

Typically the non-professional investor does research in a similar fashion, they just don't know it. They find an idea or get sent a report from a broker they walk through a series of analytics and arrive at a yes or no decision. It can be time consuming, biased and may not lead to an understanding of where the best current opportunities are.

I had for years followed a similar path of hunting for ideas ,grabbing research where I could then doing the analytics only to find after much work the stock did not make sense. I would usually find an issue on the technical side or a fundamental that was trending negatively and would all too often jettison the idea and move on. Occasionally you would find a stock that met my criteria and I would place it in the buy Column.

Given this process was time consuming and somewhat dysfunctional, I decided to take another path. With the help of a good friend, we reverse engineered the screening process and built a proprietary software platform that would grab all the key publically available data on every company in my trading universe. I would then compress all the Meta data point that met all my key criteria, producing a report with a number of names that had fully met all my Tier 1 filtering parameters.

I had gone from relying on sell side research and stumbling for ideas and names, to a systematic process for finding what was moving, why it was moving and who was buying and selling it. My universe of quality names and ideas was impressive and timely; from there I would complete the Tier 2 fundamental analysis screen and qualitative discoveries before making a buy decision.

I had developed a very efficient process where I could look at the right names and data and get a better feel for which companies I would want to take a further look at. It was a huge time saver and highly efficient targeted process. Today we make that process and the trading plan seamless through for members at www.smallcapsuccess.com.

AUTOMATION
THE NUTS AND BOLTS OF
FILTERING EFFICIENCY

Finding great ideas and stocks that are gaining traction in the market with institutional investors is fundamental to your success. However it's not always easy to find what you're looking for with all those names in the stock pages.

Premade screens available on many trading sites can be helpful but are difficult to customize the data into a meaningful report. Top hedge fund managers learn quickly to find the best ideas. They recognize you have to look in places others are not looking and act quickly when the security is beginning a breakout move. We have adopted that philosophy utilizing screening tools and custom made tracking reports to look where others may not currently be looking.

Smallcapsuccess.com clients receive detailed weekly portfolio report and specific corporate reports we view as important. We have developed and tested a process for picking small cap GARP (growth at a reasonable price) oriented stocks, which, combined with disciplined portfolio management has returned phenomenal results since our inception.

Investors can use the various screens and techniques shown in our training materials to hunt out many quality ideas that you or your advisor may wish to place in your portfolio. However we have simplified the process materially for you if you become a member.

Our proprietary data retrieval process automatically sorts out the best opportunities given our specific criteria. Automated data retrieval underpins the process by generating hundreds of stock names for review that includes colored indicators to make it easy to see which stocks are "moving." Internally we refer to this as a Tier 1 review.

Our principal habitat is the TSX and Venture Exchange (TSX)V) but U.S. exchanges are also available to us to explore when the opportunity presents.

TIER 1 PHASE 1 INFO

Symbol
Co. Name
Exchange
Volume
10 day average volume
Divident rate
Shares outstanding
Market cap
Institutional Holdings

We generate a report for small cap equity stocks that have a market cap less than $500 million. Our large cap report includes market cap of $500 million to $2 Billion.

The Phase 1 criteria selection generates a report similar to the one that is displayed below.

TIER 1 PHASE 2 INFO

Symbol
Price
Price Change
52 week high
52 week low
50 day price average
200 day price average
Industry

The Phase 2 criteria selection generates another report similar to the one that is displayed above.

The Phase 1 and 2 reports are generated for the TSX-V and TSX (TSX only for the large cap report). Overall, the raw data provides well over 1,000 names.

APPLICATION OF INDICATORS

Once the data table is clean through the small cap process we calculate the following indicators:

- **Volume Change** - this compares the most recent trading volume and compares it to the 10 day average volume. If the percentage change is > 50% we use conditional formatting to turn the cell green. If the volume is < -50% the cell turns red.

- **Price Change** - current price change over previous day is calculated: green is > 5%; red is < -5%. Anytime the price moves greater than 10% especially with volume or through a support or resistance moving average (MA) we would consider that to be material.

- **50-200 Cross** - this is a simple binary calculation that tracks whether the 50 day average has exceeded the 200 day average.

At this point we have a nice table with colorful indicators, but well over 1,000 stocks to look at. Since we are interested in the best stocks to look at we found some qualifying factors to cull the list to a more focussed list. These are the factors:

- **Average Volume Traded** - if the stock's weekly average volume is less than 15,000, we would consider it an illiquid stock, and the stock is removed from the list. This speaks to the stocks' liquidity in the market. We need at least 15,000 shares per week trading or enough volume to exit 100% of our position over the course of a week.

- **Institutional Holdings** - our experience suggests that the percentage ownership by institutions is an important factor. We eliminate stocks with less than 2% ownership and more than 40%. Too little ownership implies the company is not being followed; too much ownership means the opportunity may be too well known and valuation to rich.

- **Industry Focus** – We take a macroeconomic view of the key industry sectors and then screen for what we believe are the best opportunities. We can modify this sector list at any time to find the best opportunities given sector rotation dynamics.

Tables are distributed to clients in EXCEL allowing the users to manipulate the data. Company Names are hyperlinked to the TMX website providing the user with more information.

Data tables are formatted to print on an 81/2 X 11 if the user desires to work from paper.

We also provide select reports on specific companies on our watch or active accumulate list.

TIER 2 ANALYSIS AND TRADING:

Once the top candidates are selected we then begin a process of selecting only the best opportunities and complete our Tier 2 quantitative and qualitative analysis before engaging the trading process. Those selections end up in our weekly portfolio report.

The detailed Tier 2 analysis and trading process is available to members through webcasts and private coaching sessions. We also offer a text book for self-directed non-members.

www.smallcapsuccess.com

SMALL CAP MILLIONAIRE

SAMPLE TIER 2 REPORT:

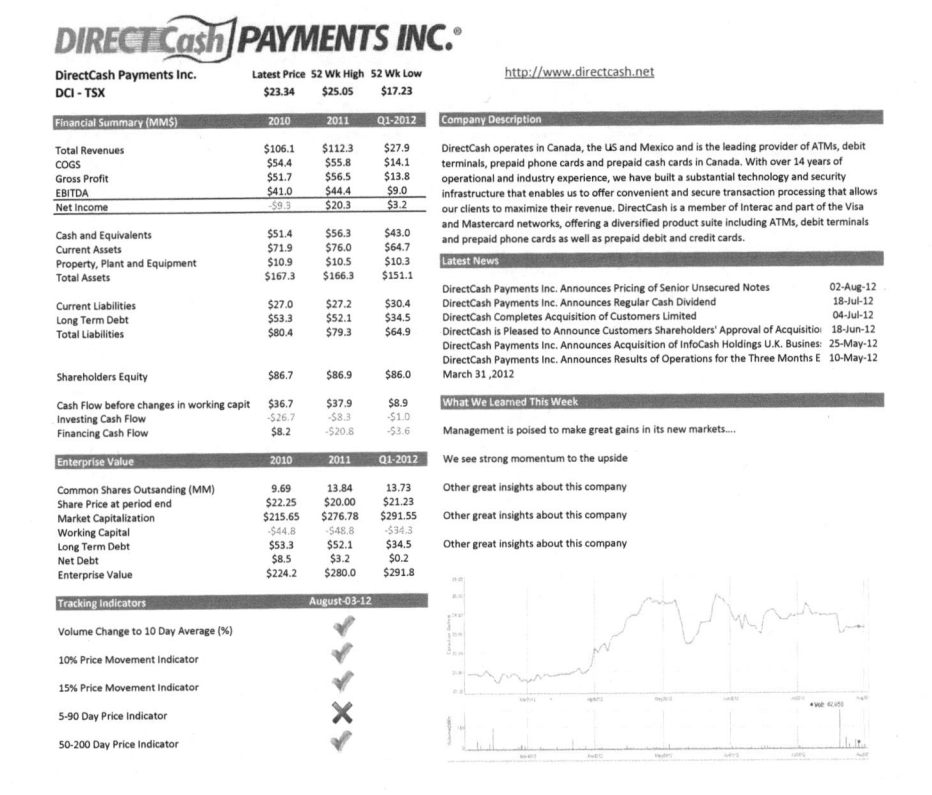

DIRECTCash PAYMENTS INC.

DirectCash Payments Inc.	Latest Price	52 Wk High	52 Wk Low
DCI - TSX	$23.34	$25.05	$17.23

http://www.directcash.net

Financial Summary (MM$)	2010	2011	Q1-2012
Total Revenues	$106.1	$112.3	$27.9
COGS	$54.4	$55.8	$14.1
Gross Profit	$51.7	$56.5	$13.8
EBITDA	$41.0	$44.4	$9.0
Net Income	-$9.3	$20.3	$3.2
Cash and Equivalents	$51.4	$56.3	$43.0
Current Assets	$71.9	$76.0	$64.7
Property, Plant and Equipment	$10.9	$10.5	$10.3
Total Assets	$167.3	$166.3	$151.1
Current Liabilities	$27.0	$27.2	$30.4
Long Term Debt	$53.3	$52.1	$34.5
Total Liabilities	$80.4	$79.3	$64.9
Shareholders Equity	$86.7	$86.9	$86.0
Cash Flow before changes in working capit	$36.7	$37.9	$8.9
Investing Cash Flow	-$26.7	-$8.3	-$1.0
Financing Cash Flow	$8.2	-$20.8	-$3.6

Company Description

DirectCash operates in Canada, the US and Mexico and is the leading provider of ATMs, debit terminals, prepaid phone cards and prepaid cash cards in Canada. With over 14 years of operational and industry experience, we have built a substantial technology and security infrastructure that enables us to offer convenient and secure transaction processing that allows our clients to maximize their revenue. DirectCash is a member of Interac and part of the Visa and Mastercard networks, offering a diversified product suite including ATMs, debit terminals and prepaid phone cards as well as prepaid debit and credit cards.

Latest News

DirectCash Payments Inc. Announces Pricing of Senior Unsecured Notes	02-Aug-12
DirectCash Payments Inc. Announces Regular Cash Dividend	18-Jul-12
DirectCash Completes Acquisition of Customers Limited	04-Jul-12
DirectCash is Pleased to Announce Customers Shareholders' Approval of Acquisitio	18-Jun-12
DirectCash Payments Inc. Announces Acquisition of InfoCash Holdings U.K. Busines	25-May-12
DirectCash Payments Inc. Announces Results of Operations for the Three Months E	10-May-12
March 31, 2012	

What We Learned This Week

Management is poised to make great gains in its new markets...

We see strong momentum to the upside

Other great insights about this company

Other great insights about this company

Other great insights about this company

Enterprise Value	2010	2011	Q1-2012
Common Shares Outsanding (MM)	9.69	13.84	13.73
Share Price at period end	$22.25	$20.00	$21.23
Market Capitalization	$215.65	$276.78	$291.55
Working Capital	-$44.8	-$48.8	-$34.3
Long Term Debt	$53.3	$52.1	$34.5
Net Debt	$8.5	$3.2	$0.2
Enterprise Value	$224.2	$280.0	$291.8

Tracking Indicators	August-03-12
Volume Change to 10 Day Average (%)	✓
10% Price Movement Indicator	✓
15% Price Movement Indicator	✓
5-90 Day Price Indicator	✗
50-200 Day Price Indicator	✓

WHAT WE SCREEN FOR AND WHY:

Let's look at some of the initial metrics we screen for. The first thing we want to do is understand the market that were looking at, where do we want to be investing and why. I call it the investing habitat or universe. If you are not comfortable investing in foreign markets, then I recommend you leave them alone. I have no competitive advantage trying to figure out what is happening in the small cap space in China; therefore it makes no sense for me to look at stocks in those markets even though I believe at a macroeconomic level there may be some great growth opportunities ahead. We stick in the market we know best and only venture out when very confident. We are principally Canadian small, mid cap and occasionally large cap in orientation. We will also look at the USA small cap universe on occasion.

There is a fine balance between too narrow a habitat and too wide. If you are to narrow you can limit your opportunities, to wide a net and you catch nothing. There is an old Chinese expression; *"He who chases two rabbits catches none"*.

Better the devil you know. There are plenty of opportunities to build wealth in the North American small cap space so that's where we look. As discussed we also prefer GARP oriented stocks and our screens are set up specifically to look at those opportunities. We will on occasion set up a specific growth screen for a particular sector if the macroeconomic view moves us there, for example, Junior Mining, but this is rare and we are very selective when we do so.

Canadian based energy companies are commonly seen in our special situation portfolios, as we have much easier access to sit down and talk to management teams directly as we reside in Calgary, Alberta. Anything we get more detailed information on can enhance our qualitative analysis and may increase the chance of a successful trade.

The second thing we look at is trading volume changes and how they compare to the 10 day average trading volume. Trading **VOLUME TO ME IS ONE OF THE KEY METRICS** we follow we only look at small cap stocks that trade at least 15,000 shares a week.

I can't tell you how many times I have been stuck in, and been whipsawed around in these thinly traded small cap stories. You need weekly trading of at least 15,000 shares to provide an appropriate level of liquidity. It should also be noted that you should never try to own more shares than you could liquidate under normal weekly volumes. For example, you purchase 5,000 shares of XYZ corp., but it only trades 1,000 shares per week on average. If you had to get out for any reason in a hurry, you have no buyers and you would be bid down to the bones to get off the stock. You would be better to own 500 shares of XYZ you could sell, than 5,000 you would get stuck on.

Material volume moving up or down is one of the early signs that individuals or institutional investors are either BUYING or SELLING the stock. Simply said volume is market interest, if the interest is good its buy volume, if the interest is bad its sell volume, if zero market interest zero volume.

Volume often moves ahead of price in many trades. We have developed a process to grab streaming daily volume and look for anomalies from the normal trading patterns of the stocks in our habitat.

SIGNIFICANT VOLUME CHANGES FROM WEEK TO WEEK OR FROM DAY-TO-DAY may be material to your decision making. If we see a stock with any abnormal weekly or daily trading volume we would identify it as a red or green flag and act accordingly by either buying or selling the stock.

It is important to note however volume is only 1 metric we use so, we would certainly look at all other key criteria before executing any trades, none the less it is a key metric we watch with great interest.

> Our volume ranges: **Volume Change -** this compares the most recent trading volume and compares it to the 10 day average volume. If the percentage change is > 50% we use conditional formatting to turn the cell green. If the volume is < -50% the cell turns red.

IF trading volume IS MOVING ,15 TO 20% either up or down from its normal weekly range we would CERTAINLY TAKE A LOOK AT IT .ONCE WE GET INTO THE 30%- 40% VOLUME changes these will get acute attention.

Recently I was looking at one of our tracking sheets and noticed a material CHANGE IN VOLUME for one of the stocks we are tracking Med Mira Inc.(MIR) TSX-V:

A 1,702% CHANGE IN VOLUME, NOW THAT got my attention and it deserved a second look just based on volume. As I looked further into my screens I noticed price indicators had not changed and it was still trading at 6 cents. The 50 day moving average had recently crossed the 200 day moving average although the price ranges were still very narrow. Weekly volume was 1.13 million shares versus 62,000 normally. That is a large block and can indicate institutional buying, but requires further investigation to find out if that is in fact the case. The 52 week low was 3 cents and the high. 7 cents, so no real break out on price. The company has 392 million shares outstanding; that's a material dilution for a small company. It also had a market cap of only 21 million dollars. Institutions held approximately 35% of its stock. Based on my general view of the volume and the number of shares outstanding I took a second look at it, curious to see what may be going on; but just over a million shares trading in a company with 392 million shares outstanding changes my view quickly, from excitement to trepidation. Ideally we like to see less shares outstanding, big volume moves along with strong price appreciation. This stock just did not fit that criterion, so we moved on.

AUTO CANADA (ACQ) TSX: A POTENTIAL BUY AND TIER 2 REVIEW

A 214% increase in volume, this was a material lift relative to its normal 10 day average volume. Although price had not moved much, the stock did manage to break out to the upside as the 50 day moving average crossed the 200 day moving average. The volume was 120,000 versus the 10 day average of 38,452. The price of $17.47 was just below its 52 week high. The stock has just fewer than 20 million shares outstanding and a market cap of 350 million. I like the fact that they had a limited amount of shares outstanding relative to their market cap. They also had strong institutional support 26%. Given the strong volume, momentum and institutional support this would meet my criteria as a potential buy and we would then proceed to a level 2 review. As you can see volume is in many ways a lead indicator, a flag that starts the process of further review. If there is no volume moving then market interest is low.

Price and moving averages: Price is dictated by the fundamentals of supply and demand.

The bid price is what someone is willing to buy the stock for, the ask price is what someone is willing to sell the stock for, the difference between the two is the bid ask spread and can be wide for small cap stocks. Larger cap highly liquid stocks generally have small bid ask spreads.

Higher demand and less supply = increase in price
Less demand and more supply = price decline

Price is a key indicator; we measure the current price, weekly changes, 50 day and 200 day moving average changes, and 52 week highs and lows.

PRICE APPRECIATION:

If the stock price is appreciating that would indicate there are more interested buyers (increased demand) and the buyers are willing to pay more given the limited supply available. We call that bidding up the stock.

Price and volume appreciation is a buy signal= Price appreciation on the back of a material volume change is confirmation of market interest.

When price is retreating that is an indication that there is less interest in the stock. There will be more available supply from the sellers than there would be demand from buyers, so the price-bid goes down.

A declining price in an indication that there is less interest in buying and less interest in the stock

We look at current price, closing price for the day, and compare that to the normal weekly and annual range and look for material variations.

How far has the price moved up or down from its normal range this week?

How far has it moved relative to its 52 week range?

Has it crossed a 50 day, or 200 day moving average?

TIER 1 PRICE AND VOLUME BUY SIGNALS:

Volume up and price appreciating more that 5% will get our attention. Price moving greater than 10% with any significant volume we would consider very material. Combined with moving average breakout to the upside (50 day moving average has crossed over the 200 day moving average- and the 9 day moving average has crossed the 50 day moving average), we would consider that to be a very material event.

Shares outstanding and market capitalization:
Shares outstanding= Number of shares issued by the company
Market capitalization= Number of shares issued X Stock price
The number of shares outstanding can vary between companies greatly. The number of shares outstanding is based on how many shares the company has issued into the market.

Generally the smaller companies have fewer shares outstanding; however, that is not always the case. When you're buying stocks you are in essence buying an equity ownership interest in the company. Ideally you want maximum revenue and a minimum number of shares issued.

SARAH AND BOB:

For example, let's say for Sarah, with the help of her accountant decided to start another business, XYZ Company. When she started the company she issued 100 shares to herself and self-funded the initial purchase. A year later XYZ has 1 million dollars in revenue and she is the only shareholder. Then 100% of the revenue is hers, and the price of her stock and market cap would reflect that.

1,000,000/100= $10,000 per share. Bear in mind this is a very simplistic view of valuation but it illustrates the point. As she owns all 100 shares herself she will own 100% of the 1 million equity value.

Bob also started his own company, BUB Company. Bob issued 100 shares to himself initially and also raised additional seed capital and sold 400 more shares to friends. Bob now has 1 million in revenues. Bob's value 1,000,000/500= $2,000 per share. Bob only owns 100 of the 500 shares outstanding resulting in $200,000 equity value, a material difference.

Sarah's equity is valued at $10,000 per share. Sarah took more initial capital risk but owns the company 100%. No shareholder issues and no dilution in equity value.

Bob's equity is valued at $2,000 per share. Bob spread some of the risk initially but it cost him dearly in the end. He owns less of the company he operates; he is also accountable to other shareholders who could vote him out as Management if he does not perform.

The bottom line: ideally the less shares outstanding and higher the share price the better your equity position. Companies that miss earning expectations and continually issue more stock and diluting your equity position are red flag companies (Bioexx comes to mind).

INSTITUTIONAL SUPPORT:

We drive this number from quarterly fund data. The percentage number indicates how much of the stock is owned by professional investors. A number less than 2 indicates there is not much formal institutional support while a number greater than 40 may mean there just too many institutions owning it and that growth may be limited.

The number is used as a guide only as the data is somewhat dated, given we receive the data at quarter's end and the managers could have made some buys or sells along the way.

We also use it as a trend indicator for stocks in the portfolio. By tracking which funds own the stocks we hold in the portfolios. If I notice that the stock has been trending down or up and the institutional indicator is also trending down or up that would be a sell or buy signal for me.

Recently we had a stock on the TSX by the name of Auto Canada (ACQ) that had a slight pullback after a big run, and I also noticed one of the funds that had held it had begun reducing their position so we adjusted by reducing ours, resulting in a nice profit and decreasing our downside risk. One of my rules is that when the big boys start to leave a story don't fight it, leave ahead of them. They have more stock to get off the table and you are more nimble, so use that to your advantage if it makes sense use the opportunity to sell.

If a stock has no institutional support it could mean a couple of things.

Firstly, it is simply too small or not developed enough for the manager to buy. Even small cap funds have targets for market capitalization, liquidity, and revenue growth. If the company is just not hitting the targets it may not be eligible to enter the fund and would be passed over not because there is no interest but because it's just not poised for growth. In some cases the company may not have mainstream fund support but if you look deeper could have some private equity support on initial financing. This could be an indication that the quality was there but the story is simply not mature enough to attract the larger fund managers. The other option is that the concept has been looked at and passed over; this is a huge red flag.

For that reason we like to see some institutional support, we like to see that a professional due diligence team has looked at the company and decided that there was in fact a good concept, solid management, earnings or earnings potential, and liquidity. We use the institutional ownership number only as a reference point to validate other metrics we are looking at.

APPLYING THE LESSONS LEARNED

- Utilize a systematic process in determining the best stock opportunities
- Volume often leads price
- Trade within your habitat
- Review institutional trading activity

Bob is looking for a small cap stock in the energy sector as he thinks the market is in the right spot for a big win in that sector. Bob should:

   a. Listen to his old buddy Al at the bowling alley for a recommendation

b. Talk to Sarah's advisor and get appropriate advice before buying any stock

c. Throw darts at the stock pages

d. Review the top five picks from the small cap success newsletter and review additional fundamental research to confirm his decision.

e. B & E

Correct answer E

Chapter #4

Fundamental Analysis of small cap stocks

THE TIER2 QUICK SCREEN

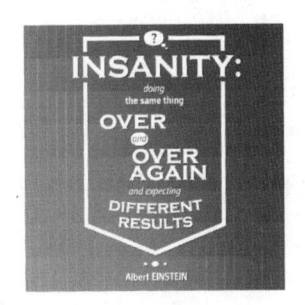

INSANITY: doing the same thing OVER and OVER AGAIN and expecting DIFFERENT RESULTS
— Albert EINSTEIN

THE ULTIMATE AUTHORITY MUST ALWAYS REST WITH THE INDIVIDUAL'S OWN REASON AND CRITICAL ANALYSIS
DALAI LAMA

LEARNING OUTCOMES:

Discover some of the most effective quantitative and qualitative strategies for assessing the fundamentals of any small cap stock.

LEARNING OBJECTIVES:

1. Examine important Tier 2 analysis tools to help you eliminate poor quality opportunities and focus on high impact plays.
2. Identify the steps involved in a Tier 2 screen
3. Evaluate various key considerations in security selection
4. Differentiate between the most commonly used technical analysis tools
5. Discover the most important fundamental balance sheet and income statement driven metrics
6. Recognize the value of a competitive analysis

Once we have filtered through our Tier 1 screen, we have likely eliminated hundreds of stocks that reside in the pages of the newspapers and stock boards. Filtering out the bad eggs or stories that are not fully mature can materially reduce your risk and add to your returns.

However this is only the first step. You will still need to complete what we call our Tier 2 analysis, which is a combination of quantitative and qualitative fundamental screening analysis techniques to further refine our search.

One must remember this is a process of elimination in an attempt to find 1-2 great ideas with the highest probability of success; filter until you find the gold nugget amongst the gravel. It is important to note that Tier 2 analysis is not fully comprehensive; it is simple quick screens around what we believe are the key drivers in these GARP stocks.

A full comprehensive fundamental analysis of the macroeconomic, microeconomic and corporate finance variables is beyond the scope of this book. However, we will review the basic elements of these factors within the Tier 2 process.

As discussed, the Tier 2 analyses is fundamentally about weeding out the bad apples further and looking for a few really good gems that you can include in the portfolio. One should look for reasons to say no to a stock, not yes. Confirmation bias is a behavioral trait that can negatively affect your stock picking ability. Individuals who have this trait tend to focus on information that confirms their existing view. If you like a stock you will look for information that confirms the positives and avoids negative information.

Think of the Tier 2 exercise as you would if you were running a series of hurdles. If you look at some information and it looks good and positive for the stock, you jump the next hurdle, you will keep jumping until the race is over and you have determined that the stock is indeed a good fit for the portfolio. After some practice you will get very good at jumping these hurdles very quickly and efficiently and before long you will have mastered the craft.

TIER 2 SCREEN TEMPLATE:

Date_____

Always a good idea to have a start date on the analysis, to be able to look back and see what has changed since you began the assessment.

Company _____ **& Ticker** _____

Market_____

Web Address_____

Company name, ticker symbol, market and web address is recorded for quick access reference.

Investor Relations Contact and Number _____

This is very important information to have, as the Investor relations contact may be able to give you additional information and insight on the current events. They can be a great source of information as you build your investment thesis.

HIGH QUALITY DIVIDEND EQUITY OR SPECULATION:

Generally a stock with dividends is more stable, but a pure growth play can afford you greater wealth building opportunity.

Is the small cap stock a high quality reliable dividend payer with growth prospects or is it a pure speculative growth story? Understanding what you're looking for is key as they can have very different risk metrics. Generally a dividend payer will tend to be more mature and stable than a pure growth play, so if you're looking at adding some yield to the portfolio to offset some pure growth risk you need to understand what you need to be searching for. Pure growth stocks will not pay a dividend; any retained earnings will generally be put right back to work expanding the business opportunity.

MARKET CAP:

Look for > than 500 million and less than 2 billion market cap.

Market capitalization is the total value of the stock. It is the stock price multiplied by the number of shares outstanding, ideally calculated on a fully diluted basis.

Generally we look for stocks with greater than 500 million in market cap and less than 2 billion (small cap). If you are too small (micro-cap <500 million market cap), many larger institutional investors cannot buy you for liquidity and other risk metric reasons, so the stock can get orphaned if the market turns on them. Because retail investors do not have these institutional risk parameters they will often get enticed into a very micro story with the hope of hitting it rich. Believe me I have been there and occasionally get moved in that direction, but it usually leads to disappointment.

Stick to small cap stocks that have some size and revenue stability to them. It will give you a much better opportunity to pick winning stocks more consistently.

Stocks under 500 million market cap but growing fast may be placed on a watch list, when they get to the 500 million range they may be included in the buy list.

THE FLOAT AND INSIDER OWNERSHIP:

Do insiders have skin in the game? Are they sellers or buyers?

The float is the total number of shares publicly owned and available for trading. The float is calculated by subtracting restricted shares from outstanding shares. It is always important to understand how the small cap company looks relative to its insiders, officers and directors.

If the insiders own very little stock it may be an indication that they have in fact sold most of the position out and you may be the next liquidity event before they pull the plug and run. It may also be an indication that management has minimal control and commitment or as we say "skin" in the game. I like to see at least 20% insider ownership, and no material selling from the board, officers or directors. Insider selling trends which you can get from SEDI or sites like Canadian insider if you're trading TSX names can be helpful in determining patterns of insider activity.

It must be recognized that the trading by insiders can occur long before the activity is reported to SEDI and made publically available; however it's the pattern of selling over time that should be a warning. I remember the Bioexx CEO was blowing out 15% of his stock on a yearly basis before the stock collapsed. Investors were asking themselves why the CEO was selling so much stock if the company has such glowing growth prospects. Of course, the CEO answered that it was simple personal financial management to clear off old liabilities, but as a business owner I knew better that something was up; it was a warning that for many went unnoticed. I trimmed my position, but in retrospect should have sold more. Large scale trading by insiders is a bad sign period. If only for the reason that the stock price hardly ever appreciates ,while the CEO or insider sells their position out. Bottom line: if they have no confidence, why should you?

CHART TREND: DAILY (UP TO 1 WEEK), 3 MONTHS, 1-3 YEARS:

Is the trend up and positive, down and negative or undeterminable-neutral?

I keep my chart analysis pretty simple. A comprehensive technical analysis view is beyond the scope of this book and certainly well beyond the scope of the quick Tier 2 analysis, however simple trend analysis can tell you a lot about the current market sentiment and give you an indication if this is a good time to buy or sell a stock.

Key considerations you should look for:

1. General trend over a day-1 week (the immediate term), 3 month (intermediate term), 1-3 year (long term), is the trend going up or down?

SMALL CAP MILLIONAIRE

This is a look at Canadian Natural Resources Limited (CNQ), the chart is compliments of www.stockwatch.com

The general trend in the last week is up, from Oct to Dec the general trend is up, although there have been significant periods of volatility. The 1 year trend has also been up.

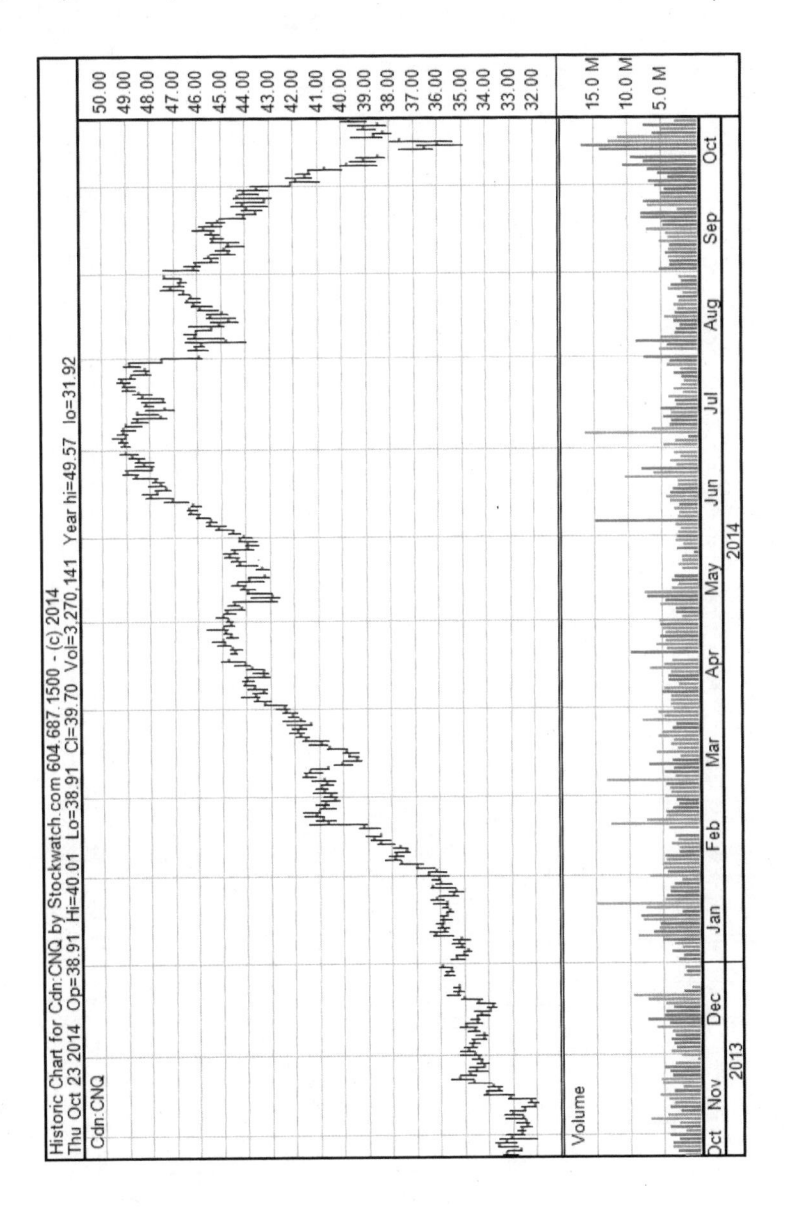

This is Wavefront Technology Solutions Inc, (WEE), you can see the trend is down and almost out. GARP investing is all about riding winning stocks higher, pure and simple. The trend is your friend when it's going north, but when it turns, time to get out. We will give you more on specific trading rules to aid in the decision making process.

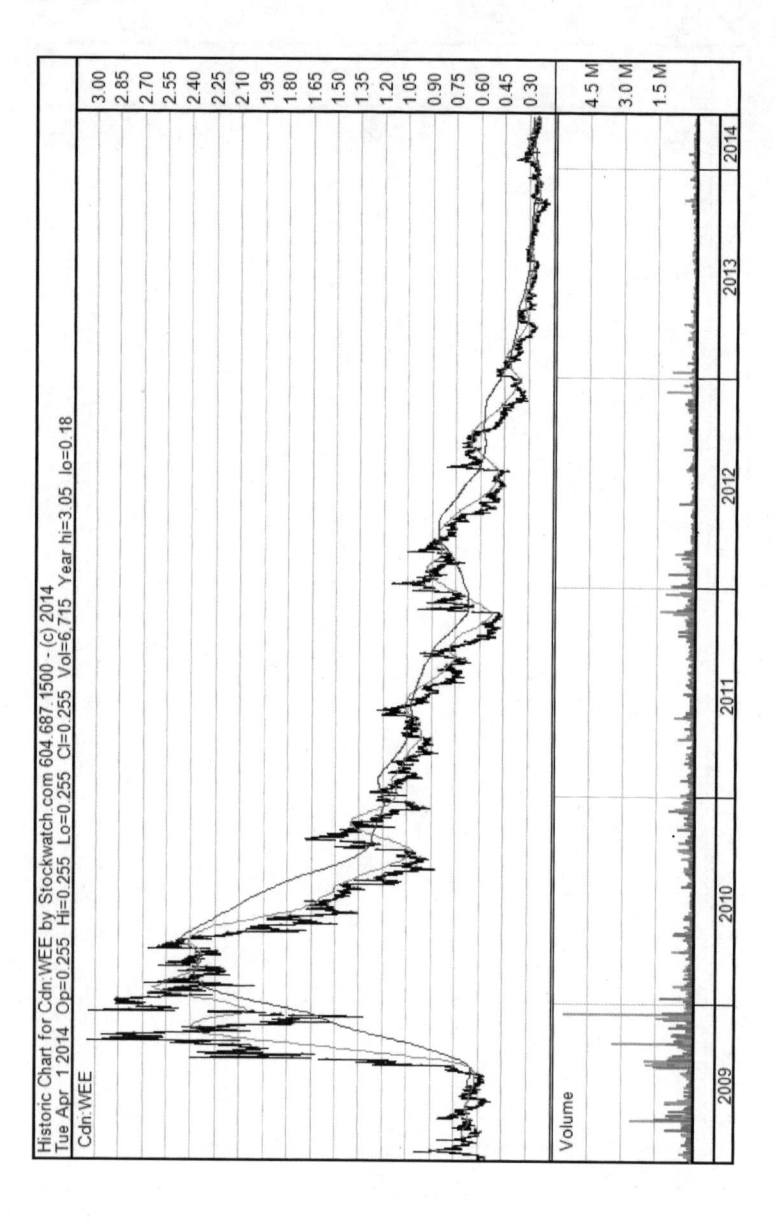

2. Moving average crosses and breakouts : *Positive up or down*

I look closely for moving average crosses and breakouts. Moving averages are a widely used indicator in technical analysis. A moving average (MA) is a trend-following or historical indicator because it is based on past prices, but it gives us a glimpse into what might happen next, as trends can and often do repeat. The two basic and commonly used MA's are the simple moving average (SMA), which is the simple average of a security over a defined number of time periods, and the exponential moving average (EMA), which gives bigger weight to more recent prices. The most common applications of MA's are to identify the trend direction and to determine support and resistance levels. While MA's are useful enough on their own, they also form the basis for other indicators such as the Moving Average Convergence Divergence (MACD). Below is another chart for Canadian Natural Resources Limited (CNQ). It is compliments of the website www.stockwatch.com; a great website for retail investors. The chart below of (CNQ) shows 3 simple moving averages and in the lower part of the chart you will see the MACD indicator.

If you look closely you can see the stock price is above the 9 day average; moving up is a good near term sign. We also have a price above the red 50 day average, again positive momentum, and we can also see in July the 50 day MA crossed over the 200 day MA to the upside, an uptrend breakout which is very positive. From the MACD perspective a 0.00 trend line is your baseline; moving above that line means positive momentum, when you drop below it means negative momentum. What we like to see is a trend from negative to positive; we can see that both 9 and 50 day have turned positive. If we put it all together the chart looks positive and has momentum in all key metrics. That said the chart only tells you part of the story and it is a historical perspective. Portfolio management is about looking forward and determining if the run will continue. If you have a positive chart and the remaining fundamentals line up, and you are buying at a decent valuation, this may be a good stock to place in the portfolio.

It is important to note that Canadian Natural Resources Limited (CNQ) would be considered a larger cap stock, so I would not place it into the small cap portion of the portfolio but it may fit into the large cap equity portfolio, or a special situations portfolio.

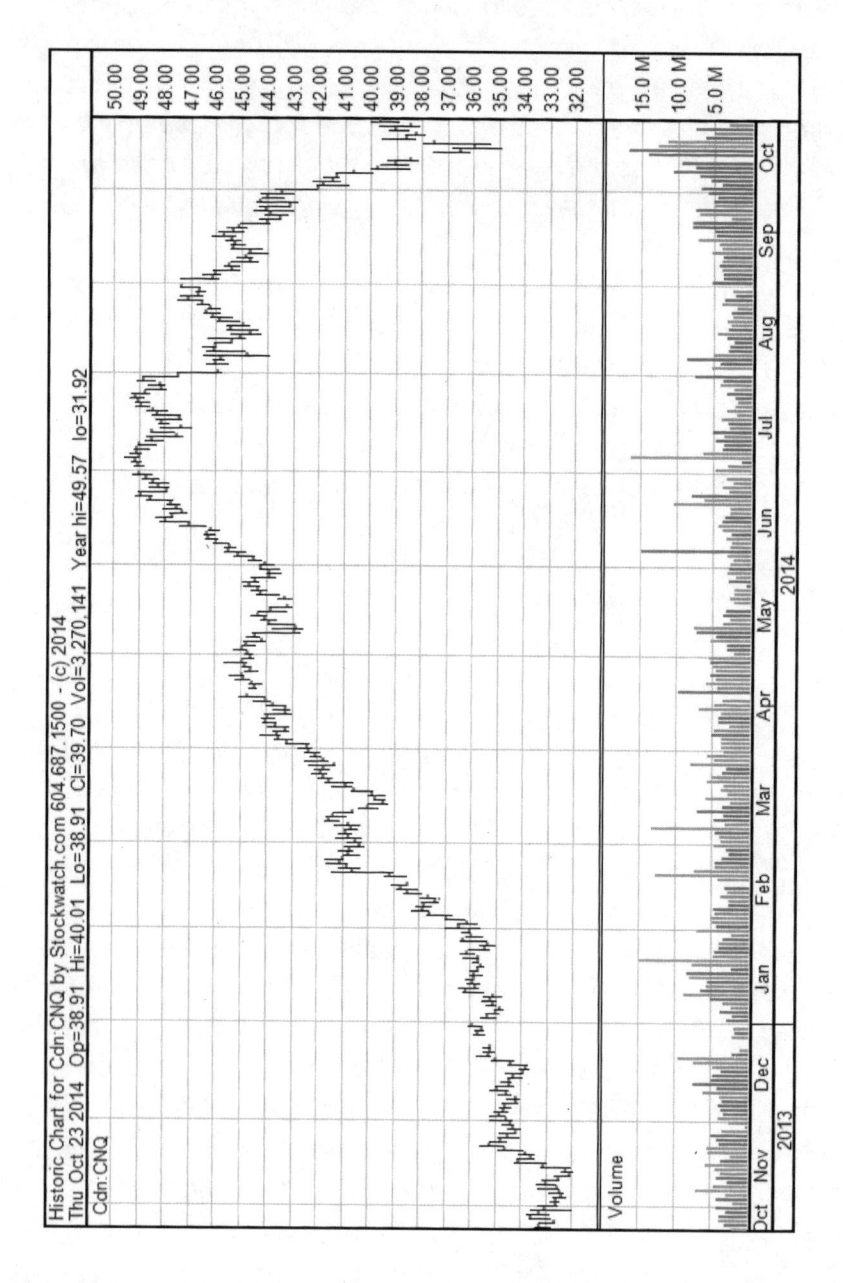

Institutional Ownership: *Net strong or weak?*

Which funds own the stock, how much do they collectively own, and have they been buyers or sellers recently?

Institutional ownership should not be the only factor in the overall decision making process but it does play a significant role. There is no question institutional buying or selling of a small cap stock can move the needle and affect the price.

The institutional players can move a stock around for a variety of reasons and the smaller retail players often get punished when they play their games. For example, Greenfields Petroleum Corporation (GNF), a stock with great long term growth prospects, has been hammered recently by 1 institution selling the stock. The word on the street is that 1 fund had a redemption issue and the sell was a forced liquidity event. Only they know for sure but the stock pays a price none–the-less. On the surface you see a weak price but only from 1 institution. The other institutions have generally held their positions and fundamentals remain unchanged. So for me it remains a hold, but a close watch for additional institutions leaving the story.

Having no institutions owning the stock may be a bad sign; it could indicate 2 things. One, they have looked and passed, or two, they have not seen the story yet, which may indicate that it is still a very micro concept only and not ready for institutional investors. Either way it means risk, and you should consider that in the decision making process. What's worse is a stock that has had strong institutional support in the past and then it all disappeared. This is a huge red flag and should be taken seriously.

I like to see between 2-40% institutional support; I flag this number from a variety of sources including Morningstar. Support of 2% means someone has looked at the story and has determined that it has met minimal institutional level due diligence and decided to buy. A number greater than 40 % may indicate that the cat is already out of the bag and most institutions now hold it; the easy money may be gone.

Idea Generation: *Strong reliable source or weak?*

Where you find the story really does matter. I like to keep track of where we are finding our portfolio ideas. Most come directly from our proprietary screens and we also have some industry specific picks we add to our special situation portfolio.

Ask yourself did you get turned onto the story from a proprietary process like www.smallcapsuccess.com or other technical newsletter? Was it a newspaper, trade journal, TV, internet or an uninformed tip from a friend?

The closer you are to the story the better. The great portfolio manager Peter Lynch used to do very fundamental on the ground sleuth research to uncover some great investment ideas. He would sit for hours in malls to see what the kids were buying, identifying new trends early and taking advantage of them.

I have found that specific industry knowledge can be material in picking great winners. Athabasca Oil Corporation (ATH) is a great example. I got into that story very early on, with a private placement investment just as the Alberta oil sands story was emerging.

We use a proprietary filtering process to stream ideas in our general portfolio, followed by a detailed sector analysis, where we often go out to friends in industry and ask them what they think of the company. That on the ground knowledge has saved me on many occasions.

Generally speaking the broader the awareness of the story, the weaker the opportunity. In fact many of those stock market focused television shows that have those talking heads picking winners is a sure fire strategy to have your pocket picked. Just be aware one person's top pick today is also likely to be his liquidity event when you jump on and buy the recommendation.

News Reports, Bulletins, Press releases: *Net positive or negative?*

I like to keep track of any recent press releases, bulletins, or news reports on the stories we are considering or have in the portfolio. Most of the stocks we select will have an alert process for their news releases that you can sign up for and they will send them directly to you. It's critical to stay abreast of any new material events and act on them. At www.smallcapsuccess.com, we and our clients also have immediate access to the trading activity linked to the stocks we follow or have in the portfolio, which helps us make timely portfolio management decisions.

The Economic view: *Macro & Micro, net positive or net negative?*

As a teacher of both Macro and Micro economics I have long recognized the value of catching both the big picture while keeping an eye on the small details that in many ways drive the markets and individual stock valuations.

You may not have a desire to teach economics like I do, but you should understand that a big part of our analysis and success is based on gaining a better understanding of both the micro and macroeconomic drivers of future growth, which in my experience can drive a stock price long term.

Microeconomics is the study of decisions that people and individual businesses make regarding the allocation of resources and prices of goods and services. This means also taking into account taxes and regulations created by governments. Microeconomics focuses on supply and demand and other forces that determine the price levels seen in the economy. For example, microeconomics would look at how a specific company could maximize production and its capacity so it could lower prices and better compete in its industry.

Looking at an individual company from a microeconomic view has significant value. Understanding how they make money, who is buying their products, what is the current demand level and trend can have a significant impact in the small cap space. If we see a significant consumer preference shift, a trend away from a product or slowing sales, this will lead to an earnings slowdown and likely a selloff in the stock.

Macroeconomics is the field of economics that studies the behavior of the economy as a whole and not just on specific companies, but entire industries and economies. This looks at economy-wide phenomena, such as gross domestic product (GDP) and how it is affected by changes in unemployment, national income, rate of growth, and price levels. The macro view tells us about the world around us; big macro trends, how things are shaping up in the longer term.

Identifying broad macro shifts and themes are critical to your success as an investor. One example would be the natural gas market in North America. Not too long ago Canada was in a fantastic space in terms of being on the verge of becoming a real global energy giant. Natural gas domestically was trading around $12.00MCF, Oil $90.00+ per barrel with the USA demanding the entire product mix we could ship to them.

Canada and the Canadian energy giants like Encana and Suncor were unstoppable. As Malcolm Gladwell would say, the "Goliaths of industry." Then like a thief in the night, Packers Plus hit the street with a new down hole fracking technology and the energy world changed.

Oil and Gas fields that had previously not been exploitable were now being opened up. We now had more gas than we knew what to do with it. The drilling trend extended to the south, with the USA exploiting its own tight reservoirs, making itself a leading energy producer once again.

That is a macro trend if you missed it, or if you failed to react to it you perished. If you were able to jump on board early and recognize what was happening you made millions investing in both the resource companies and service companies supporting the drilling.

"Keeping your eyes on both the small, and big picture matters".

Sector view, Performance and Outlook over last 3-6-12 Months: Net Bullish, Bearish, Neutral?

Sector analysis falls under the macro view, being in a good story and the wrong sector can lead to material disappointment and portfolio underperformance unless you're a long term contrarian investor.

Many growth portfolio managers today practice active sector rotation, meaning they will leave one sector that is slowing for a sector they believe will outperform. In simple terms portfolio managers are opportunists at heart, they have no issues with leaving the sweet girl they came to the dance with for one they feel offers them a better short term opportunity for the evening. They may return someday to that sweet young lady, but not tonight; they have another easier target in sight.

When the industry consensus was that the Canadian energy market will be soft, the managers harshly and brutally rotated away from Canadian energy and into another sector that is moving. If you were caught in an all Canadian Energy portfolio you were dead. Having a view of what sectors are moving and where the economy is headed is key to your success.

Interest rate and Inflation Trend: Strong growth environment or weak

This core basic economic data around interest rate and inflation trends is available from many sources including Stats Canada, or the Bank of Canada. In the USA, the Federal Reserve or a number of industry sources and websites including yahoofinance.com. We also provide in our newsletter our macro view of the world and micro view of individual securities.

Believe me there is no shortage of economic opinion, the challenge is even the best analysts cannot predict the future with certainty. I like to look at sites like PIMCO asset management and major financial websites like Bloomberg and Reuters and form my own opinion. These sites have some of the top industry experts looking at the key macro trends globally.

Generally low interest rates and low inflation are good for growth. Rising inflation and interest rates are seen as a weight on the economy and the stock market, especially stocks and investments with a fixed yield component. Currently we are at historically low interest rates and have until recently seen central banks in a very expansionary Keynesian mood, but that will likely change, and when it does investors must act and act fast.

Analyst Ratings & Forecasts: *Positive or negative sentiment?*

I find that most sell side analysts or pure promote newsletter analysts have so many conflicts of interests relative to the stocks they cover that their opinion is of little to no value in terms of trading recommendations. The analysis can provide some value from a pure data perspective but you should take the view that the larger pension funds and institutional buy side mangers have done their own independent analysis to form an opinion. If you are able to get an initiation report or updates from the sell side managers so be it; they have some value in terms of understanding the core business, but from that point on it's up to you as an individual investor to put on your skeptical hat and form your own opinion. Just remember, sell side analysts are there to support the corporate banking group and help them generate fees for the firm, so the research is always biased. A word about analyst ratings: You will see a variety of ratings but the general context is the same, the top pick rating is a "strong buy" and "underperform" is essentially a sell which is almost never seen and means "get out now." You may see terms like outperform or market perform; do not let those terms confuse you, simply look at their rating scale on the report and determine where the term lines up. If the recommendation is top pick, then it's a strong buy and it's worth a look. "Market perform" or lower is another way of saying sell. Speculative is just that; speculation with higher than normal risk and the analyst is not sure how to model the earnings or future earnings yet so they call it speculative.

Sentiment Indexes: *Positive or negative?*

A number of websites including Morningstar may post a variety of sentiment indexes. A sentiment index it is graphical or numerical indicator designed to show how a group feels about a stock or an economic variable. The sentiment indexes I like to follow show me how the large fund managers see the stock in terms of their buying and selling activity. This can give you some insight as to institutional buying. A positive sentiment indicator is generally a good sign. Other sentiment indicators such as a consumer or purchasing manager index may give you a macroeconomic view as to the broad economy.

The Income statement and balance sheet Fundamentals

Understanding the basics of the income statement and balance sheet are essential for any investor. The explanation I provide is by no means a detailed explanation of all the accounting variables one may look at as they review a company, However it will give the investor the core variables I look at when making a buy or sell decision.

I always start my analysis by looking at the income statement with a look at the top line revenue number. No revenue, walk away, run, run , run. We do not buy concept stocks period. If the company has no revenue and no growth profile to model I walk away. I cannot tell you how many times I have been burned by these small cap concept stocks.

Small cap CEO: Concept Company

"Earnings will show up next quarter. Don't worry, we're close; be patient almost there. We just need to get over this next hurdle and we believe we will have positive cash flow."

I would much rather see we a company who demonstrates they have future earnings using a forecast of that is based on actual sales. Talk is cheap! If the company can't model the earnings then they shouldn't have your money.

Earnings Growth expectation: *Positive or negative?*

First and foremost a company has to have positive earnings and a positive growth outlook. I like to see at a minimum 20% organic growth in the top line revenue number year over year, but 30-40% is ideal. Too much growth too quickly can certainly look positive upfront however it may also have negative elements if not managed well. One should ask management how they will manage growth if it materially exceeds expectation; if there is no plan to manage the growth, exit the stock.

I also look closely at where the growth is coming from: is it 1 customer or is broad growth across a number of customers? The more clients and the broader the product mix, the stronger the earnings. Any slowing in the top line revenue number should be looked at closely.

EPS: *Positive or negative?*

The Earnings per Share measure is one of the most commonly used metrics for growth forecasts. It is defined as the portion of a company's profit allocated to each outstanding share of a common stock. The bottom line Earnings per share (EPS), is an indicator of a company's profitability, it is usually front and centre on any analyst report.

Calculated as:

$$\frac{\text{Net Income - Dividends on Preferred Stock}}{\text{Average Outstanding Shares}}$$

When calculating, it is more accurate to use a weighted average number of shares outstanding over the reporting term, because the number of shares outstanding can change over time. However, data sources sometimes simplify the calculation by using the number of shares outstanding at the end of the period. Diluted EPS expands on basic EPS by including the shares of convertibles or warrants in the outstanding shares number.

PEG RATIO: POSITIVE OR NEGATIVE?

The PEG ratio is an effective tool for a quick snapshot of valuation. When buying stocks you should ask yourself if you are underpaying or overpaying relative to consensus growth forecasts. Ideally you want to be underpaying today for positive future growth, but how do you tell? One metric is the PEG ratio.

The PEG ratio is the Price Earnings ratio divided by the expected growth rate.

$$\frac{\text{P/E ratio} \div \text{analyst forecast estimate}}{\text{Annual expected Growth rate}}$$

The forecasted growth rate (based on the consensus of professional analysts) and the forecasted earnings over the next 12 months are used to calculate the PEG.

In theory, the lower the PEG ratio the better - implying that you are paying less for future earnings growth. Value-oriented investors like warren Buffet pay close attention to this ratio. The theory is that all an investor is really buying is future earnings growth. If you're paying too much for that growth, when the P/E rate exceeds the growth rate, is considered a bad sign.

PE/RATIO: POSITIVE OR NEGATIVE?

The PE ratio is a valuation ratio of a company's current share price compared to its per-share earnings. Calculated as:

$$\frac{\text{Market Value per Share}}{\text{Earnings per Share (EPS)}}$$

For example, if a company is currently trading at $45 a share and earnings over the last 12 months were $1.85 per share, the P/E ratio for the stock would be 24.30 ($45/$1.85)

EPS is usually from the last four quarters (trailing P/E), but sometimes it can be taken from the analyst's estimated earnings expected in the next four quarters (projected or forward P/E). A third variation uses the sum of the last two actual quarters and the estimates of the next two quarters.

Also sometimes known as "earnings multiple."

In general, a high P/E suggests that investors are expecting higher earnings growth in the future compared to companies with a lower P/E. It's usually more useful to compare the P/E ratios of one company to other companies in the same industry, and to the market in general or against the company's own historical P/E. It would not be useful for investors using the P/E ratio as a basis for their investment to compare the P/E of a technology company (high P/E) to a utility company (low P/E) as each industry has much different growth prospects.

The P/E is sometimes referred to as the "multiple", because it shows how much investors are willing to pay per dollar of earnings. If a company were currently trading at a multiple (P/E) of 30, the interpretation is that an investor is willing to pay $30 for $1 of current earnings.

- Generally a high P/E ratio means that investors are anticipating higher growth in the future.

Sales Growth>15-25%: *Growing or shrinking?*

This is a key metric for me; if sales growth is not organic, then it is likely being fed through acquisition (at best) or fraud (at worst). Consensus sales forecasts may be seen on analyst reports or by reading carefully through the company's MD&A (management discussion and analysis). I recall analyzing a company called Wavefront Technology Solutions, Inc. The company had sliding sales growth and revenue was dropping fast until they acquired another company. The newly acquired revenues were incorporated into their financials to show sales growth. The fact is the company was poorly run and the new acquisition was overly expensive and did not add meaningful long term value to the company.

Always look at the basics; what do they sell, how many have they sold, how many do they expect to sell next quarter, are they growing, who are the clients that are buying, when do they get paid, and what are the profit margins?.

Keep the process basic; if there is no organic sales with decent margins then the business will fail. Whether you're running a lemonade stand or a billion dollar oil and gas Service Company, the same basics apply; no sales with a healthy profit margin and the company will eventually perish.

Profit Margins & Trend: *Growing or shrinking?*

When you buy a share in a company what you're really buying is the ability of the management team to demonstrate they can produce profits and drive shareholder value.

The greater the profits the greater the wealth creation effect and the more economic value you will be able to receive at a point in the future.

Profit margin is calculated as net income divided by revenues, or net profits divided by sales. It measures how much out of every dollar of sales a company actually keeps in earnings. From those earnings a company has 2 choices in terms of allocating those earnings, either send monies out as a dividend to shareholders or retain it inside the company for investing in further growth opportunities.

Profit margin is useful when comparing companies in similar industries. A higher profit margin indicates a more profitable company that has better control over its costs compared to its competitors. Profit margin is displayed as a percentage; a 20% profit margin, for example, means the company has a net income of $0.20 for each dollar of sales.

The higher the profit margin, a higher chance the business will succeed; a shrinking margin means higher risk. What is important is the trend, Research in Motion Limited, the maker of Blackberry, is a former tech giant that only a short 5 years ago commanded a huge market share and significant margins but is now on the verge of irrelevancy. Margin compression and slowing sales and earnings will in eventually bring down any business, even a giant like the maker of Blackberry.

Earnings surprise History: *Surprises: yes or no?*

Any negative earnings surprise is a negative sign, no matter how hard management or sell side analysts try to spin it. I run by the cockroach theory; there is never just one, so when you see a material miss on the earnings front it's a huge warning to get out. Take a look at recent trading from insiders and the funds. If you see these investors exiting the stock and then announce an earnings surprise, it's definitely time to get out of the investment.

Debt to Equity: *Appropriate use of debt?*

Any company that carries too much debt relative to its earning strength will get itself into trouble. Understanding how much debt a company has and its ability to cover any debt obligations is a key financial metric. When looking at the debt/equity ratio you have to look at the industry in which the company operates to determine if the level is offside with what is considered normal. For example, capital-intensive industries such as larger scale manufacturing tend to have a debt/equity ratio above 2 to finance things such as inventory, while computer software companies tend to have a lower debt/equity ratio usually under 0.5.

A measure of a company's financial leverage calculated by dividing its total liabilities by stockholders' equity. It indicates what proportion of equity and debt the company is using to finance its assets.

$$\frac{\textbf{Total Liabilities}}{\textbf{Shareholders Equity}}$$

A high debt/equity ratio generally means that a company has been aggressive in financing its growth with debt. This can result in volatile earnings as a result of the additional interest expense. If a lot of debt is used to finance increased operations (high debt to equity), the company could potentially generate more earnings than it would have without this outside financing. If this were to increase earnings by a greater amount than the debt cost (interest), then the shareholders benefit as more earnings are being spread among the same amount of shareholders. However, the cost of this debt financing may outweigh the return that the company generates on the debt through investment and business activities and become too much for the company to handle. This can lead to bankruptcy, which would leave shareholders with nothing.

CASH AND CASH EQUIVALENTS ON THE BALANCE SHEET

Can the company cover short term liabilities or is it cash starved?

Balance sheet cash and cash equivalents fall under short term assets on the balance sheet; it can be a subjective metric. Too much cash sitting idle on the balance sheet and not being used to grow the business can be seen as a bad thing and point to mismanagement. Having not enough cash or equivalents can lead to an inability to cover short term liabilities and could force the sale of other revenue generating assets at an inappropriate time. I like to see at least 1 year of normalized operating expenses covered in cash or cash equivalents. When a company has less than 12 months of cash left on the balance sheet, especially with declining revenue or slow sales is a big red flag. The company will only have a few choices if it can't cover those short term liabilities, and none of them are good making them extremely vulnerable. The company could dilute shareholders and sell more equity, take on more debt, cut expenses or sell assets; either way the share price will get punished.

Burn rate and survival: You need 12 months at least

Always look at how much cash a company has, what their normalized or expected operating expenses (burn rate) are for the year and make sure they can survive at least the next 12 months or exit the stock.

Example:

ABC Company has 1 million dollars in cash on the balance sheet and is currently burning 1 million dollars per quarter.

Will they survive 12 months?

Answer = No

Your action: **sell and redeploy capital to a stronger alternative**

Free Cash Flow: *Positive yes or no?*

A company cannot expand, grow and take advantage of market opportunities if it is not generating positive cash flow. Free cash flow is a measure of financial performance calculated as operating cash flow less capital expenditures.

Earnings Before Tax (EBT) + Depreciation & Amortization - Change in Net Working Capital - Capital Expenditure. It can also be calculated by taking operating cash flow and subtracting capital expenditures. Generally speaking, the higher the free cash flow the healthier the company.

EARNINGS DRIVERS RATIONAL:

Are the earnings drivers fundamentally strong?

Understanding that core earnings drivers are critical, most businesses have core earnings drivers that account for the majority of earnings, so understanding what they are and how the market or competitive products may affect them is very important to long term growth assumptions.

Key questions I like to ask management:

SWOT analysis of earnings: Strengths, weakness, opportunities and threats.

1. What is the strength of your earnings? How did your company make money last year, what products did they sell, has there been any change to the product mix?_____

2. How did you make money last quarter? What was the top selling product and why? Do you expect those sales to continue or grow? Do you see any future weakness to those earnings?_____

3. Are these high or low quality earnings? Broad and deep market? Are there significant barriers to entry? Do we see new high value products being added to the product mix?___

4. What's Forces tend to move the sector? How do you plan to take advantage of future opportunities to grow earnings?___

5. Company Comparisons; who is a competitive threat?_____

Current Price & consensus 12 month Target Price based on PE and Earnings per Share forecast:

Current_____ **Target** _____

From the analysis provided, an investor should work out a basic forecast and projected future share price or target share price.

Target Price = P/E x EPS

You can establish a basic sensitivity estimate by determining a low and high range.

Example: XYZ Corp
25 x 1.48 = 37.00 low
35 X 1.48 = 52.00 high

COMPETITIVE ANALYSIS:

Do we have material competitive threats or do we have significant barriers to entry?

I like to have a basic understanding of a company's absolute or perceived competitive advantage. It can often be the difference between winning or losing on a trade.

A competitive analysis is a critical part of your evaluation process especially if the company has a new or novel technology. In fact I would say without reservation the more complex the technology the greater your due diligence has to be relative to the competition. I will always look to outside specialists to help me in the evaluation if required although having a clinical science background can be beneficial in utilizing a scientific methodology in my evaluations.

One of the key things I look at is what is the company trying to do in terms of the scale of the endeavour and who might they dislodge if they are successful.

The larger the endeavour and the greater the stakes the more fierce the competition will be. Some competitors are simply too big to compete against and the market entry very difficult for a new small cap company. The big dogs will fight like rabid animals to protect market share. I have a number of examples of good companies with interesting technology but they underestimated the challenges they faced in going up against a strong and fierce competitor once they began to chew out even minimal market share.

An effective approach in evaluating the company's competitors is by placing them in strategic groups according to how directly they compete for a share of the customer's dollar and doing a basic SWOT analysis.

(Strength, weakness, opportunities, threats).

For each competitor or strategic group, examine their product or service, profitability, growth, marketing objectives and assumptions, current and past strategies, cost structure, strengths and weaknesses, and size (in sales) of the competitor's business. Answer questions such as:

- Who are the top 3-5 competitors?
- What products or services do they sell, are they the same or very similar?
- What is each competitor's market share?
- What are their current and past strategies, how strong are they?
- What are each competitor's strengths and weaknesses?
- How much capital will it take to compete against them?
- If we are undercapitalized relative to the competition what is the risk to my investment and the company?

Include such things as target market, price, size, method of distribution, and extent of customer service for a product. For a service, list prospective buyers, where the service is available, price, website, toll-free phone number, and other features that are relevant. A glance at the competition will help you see where your company's product fits in the overall market and the barriers to entry.

The Bottom line: if the company in question is too small, and to under-capitalized the company will likely fail a head to head fight with a strong competitor.

The Business Plan, Investor Presentations, & Conference Calls:

Positive and professional or weak and unprofessional?

All businesses worth looking at should be able to provide you some kind of basic business plan and strategy by way of a formal document No matter how they deliver the strategy to you these are some of the key factors you should review.

Management Team, Key Executives, Board Quality, Clean Accounting and Governance: *positive or negative occurrences?*

The success or failure of any company directly leads back to management. Poor quality and a sketchy past track record have a low probability of success, no matter how good the investment sounds.

1. *Who is the management team, what is the experience level, have they had past success in the current industry or another industry?*
2. *Who are the key executives and if one of them should leave what might happen to the company?*
3. *What is the quality of the board and how are they incentivized in terms of compensation?*
4. *Have there ever been any accounting irregularities?*
5. *What are your corporate governance and code of conduct policies; any violations with any of them in this or other companies?*

The stronger the Management team the better your chances of a successful investment. Look at what they have done, less what they say they are going to do.

Strategic Investors, Partners and Contracts: *positive and significant or window dressing?*

Does the company have any key strategic investors, partners, or material contracts that will give them an advantage in the future or are they weak and strike you as "window dressing" appointments?

Growth requires a number of elements including sound products offered and competitive prices, but also considerable capital investment and quality management. The better the strategic partners, investors and contracts the greater the likelihood for sustained growth.

KEY QUESTIONS YOU WANT TO SEE ANSWERED IN THE BUSINESS PLAN, MD&A OR ON A CONFERENCE CALL:

a. *How did the company make money last year?*_____

b. *How did it make money Last Quarter?*_____

c. *Are these high or low quality earnings?*_____

d. *What forces tend to move the sector?*_____

e. *How has the stock performed? Last year, last 3 months, last month, last week, TREND*_____

f. *Company Comparisons, who is a threat?*_____

g. *What are the comparable PE and PEG ratios? Is it expensive or cheap relative to a competitor?*_____

h. *How much debt do they carry? How long can they survive? (Burn Rate)*_____

i. *How much debt is due this year, and can they survive with current cash flow?*_____

NOTES ON ADDITIONAL COMMENTS:

_____
_____
_____
_____
_____
_____
_____
_____

INVESTOR RELATIONS AND TV TALK SHOW COMMENTARY: POSITIVE OR PURE PROMOTE?

Investor relations (IR) firms are paid by a company to gain market exposure for their clients and spin the story in favour of management always. Take anything the IR firm says with a grain of salt. That said they can be a very valuable resource for the smaller public companies looking for continuous exposure in a very crowded and noisy market place. There are a number of high quality IR firms that offer tremendous value to their corporate clients and occasionally you can obtain a timely nugget of information if you get to know them. The most important thing is to determine if the IR firm is a bona fide and reputable IR firm or simply a stock promotion entity. The bona fide firm is worthy of your time.

As I said on occasion you may obtain a nugget of information from the IR firm that can be of value. Selective disclosure is of course frowned upon by the industry but it does happen. Just be aware when these guys decide to selectively disclose, the information you receive may not be credible. In fact you may be being used as liquidity cover for an investor looking to exit the stock. Another consideration is whether the information is in fact material. If it is material and not publically known it would be considered inside information and you would be wise not to trade on that knowledge.

Another source of sketchy information that the retail investor tends to lap up comes from the TV portfolio manager pundit. These guys are masters at subtle selective disclosure and they do this with great regularity and sophistication. It's a subtle pump and dump, but "pump and dump" none the less.

Always do your own independent evaluation before trading and if you're not a confident self-directed investor talk to a reputable qualified Investment advisor or portfolio manager before you make any trade.

APPLYING THE LESSONS LEARNED

- *Analyzing stocks is like jumping a series of hurdles; jump 1 data point at a time, until you have cleared all the obstacles in your path.*

- *Complete all the analysis you need to make a quality decision, especially a buy decision.*

- *Never be afraid to walk away when things do not look right*

- *Watch what the institutions are doing but think and act independently based on your own opinion*

- *Fundamentals matter but the tape never lies, when you see clear warning signs on the technical side act.*

Bob has been looking at a stock for a while and contemplating whether to buy some shares.

While returning from his Mexican vacation he had been reading an article about a new tech company. Bob loves new tech start-ups; this company claims to use electricity to clean contaminated water in a more efficient way. The company has no earnings; any patents it claims to have are very weak; no real novel technology but a slight innovation in process, less than 1 million cash in the bank, commonly issues new shares to unsophisticated investors and trades on the Over the Counter (OTC) markets. Since it is a heavily promoted stock by the CEO, the article was actually paid advertising.

   a. Buy all he can get

   b. Walk away as this story meets none of the key criteria small cap success recommends.

   c. Talk to the CEO, and after he tells you he sees orders soon, buy the stock ahead of the market.

   d. Talk to an advisor and see if you can obtain some independent research before making a decision.

Correct answer: B, although you may be enticed to look at some independent or unbiased research, I doubt you will find any:, it will likely be paid for research commonly referred to as a pump and dump scheme. Pump and dump is a strategy where company insiders issue stock to themselves cheaply then sell the stock later at much higher prices to an ill-informed public. PUMP the stock up then DUMP the shares. There are much better opportunities in the market to apply your time and energy.

Chapter #5

The Trading Plan

BUYING AND SELLING SMALL CAP STOCKS

LEARNING OUTCOME:

Analyze the core elements for buying and selling small cap stocks

LEARNING OBJECTIVES:

1. Recognize and apply the key buying and selling strategies for small cap stocks

2. Compare and contrast red flags and green flags for small cap stock trading

3. Differentiate between long and short trading strategies

4. Calculate pre trade risk metrics

5. Recognize and differentiate when and how to use the non-negotiable trading rules

THE TRADING PLAN:

The trading plan is the last and certainly most crucial piece of the FABS process; it is the when to buy and when to sell a stock.

The process of what to buy, what to avoid and when to sell a stock are what I call the trading plan; they are all interlinked and of equal importance.

When I look to buy a stock I walk through a process of looking for those positive green flags and weigh them against the red flags. Each green flag carries a weight in terms of importance; as you can see from the green flags below some items carry more weight than others.

I total the score at the end of the section and then move forward to the red flags. I also use the red flags and things to avoid as part of my reassessment and sell parameters when I own a position. For a solid buy I have to have a high degree of certainty in terms of green flags over red flags and at least a score 70% higher green then red. As you can see, there are a number of red flag areas that are heavily weighted. A few key red flags will essentially eliminate you buying a stock, which is the whole point here. Again, it's further elimination and filtering to find that gem and put the probability of success in your favour.

Even with all the filtering screening and calculating you are likely to guess wrong 50-70% of the time, and that is why it is critical to exit those positions early and let the winners run. You can have a highly efficient portfolio by maintaining even a 30%/70% win loss ratio if the winners are allowed to run and the losers are sent packing early.

WHAT TO BUY:

- Increasing Sales Growth (1 point);
- Increasing Earnings Trends (2 points);
- Increasing Margins (1 point); Ascending chart trend (2 points);
- Increased volume and price driven by increasing institutional buying (2 points);
- Breakout to the upside 9 day past 50 day (3 points);
- Moving Average 50 past 200 Moving Average (3 points);
- Positive volume and price increase with a 50 day MA cross (3 points);
- Positive 200 Day Moving Average (2 points);
- Positive MACD signs (1 point);
- Positive press releases (1 point);
- Consensus earnings forecast positive (1 point);

- Positive analyst sentiment (1 Point).

Total score and comments:

_____
_____
_____
_____

WHAT TO AVOID AND WHEN TO SELL

***CEO lying to investors

*** Restated earnings

***Large unexpected selling forcing a Gap down, and blowing through a 50 or 200 day MA support level.

*** Unexpected or unexplained material selling by key officers and directors

- Negative Regulatory Filings TSX, ASC, SEDAR, EGDAR(-4 points);
- Slowing Sales Growth (-1 point);
- Increasing Inventories (-1 point);
- Unexpected Capital Expenditures (-1point);
- Shrinking Margins (-2 points);
- Insider Trading (-5 points);
- Excessive Short Positions (-2 points);
- Increased Institutional Volume on the sell side (-3 points);
- Negative Press releases (-3 points);

- Unexpected CEO/CFO resignations or management changes (-6 points);
- Continuous officers and directors selling down the stock (-4 points).

TECHNICAL PATTERNS:

- Descending chart trend (-3 points);
- Reverse Head and Shoulders (-3 points);
- 52 Week high hitting resistance with slowing volume (-2 points);
- Breakout to the downside past the 50 day support line and 200 day Moving Average (-5 points);
- Negative MACD Signs (-3 points);

*Total score and comments:*_____

_____
_____
_____
_____

PUTTING IT ALL TOGETHER:

Total green flags_____
Total Red Flags_____
Buy_____ **Watch list** _____ **Sell** _____

If 70% more green flags than red and no critical issues (***) then place the stock on the buy or watch list.

Current Price_____ **50% trim target**_____
12-24 month exit Target_____

If the investor determines it is a buy, then determine the current price for the stock and ask yourself if it is a good value at that price; if so make the trade.

When you have a significant gain of 30-40% or more you may consider trimming 50% of the position. Certainly if your gain is greater than 100% you would automatically trim 50%. Do not be a pig, as they have a tendency to get slaughtered. Remember buying a stock is the easy part, selling it at a profit or selling in the face of a loss is very difficult. Always follow the trading rules on the sell side as they are there to protect you from your behavioural biases.

Hold Period Trading Timeline Rational: *1-3 year*

Generally I like to look at stocks from the perspective of giving them at least 1-3 years to develop and grow. I am not a big fan of day trading; I think there are just too many short term variables that can move the market and force you into selling a good story much too soon. I am also not a big fan of the buy and hold forever strategy, if the stock is screaming to be sold or (as we say) the tape has turned against you then to hold on makes no sense to me. We are momentum GARP investors. When the tide turns against you it is better to move on to a story that is moving in the right direction. So in essence I like stocks that have established themselves and proven they can make money but also have room to develop new markets.

Most stocks move in market cap tranches as they grow, and different institutional investors with different mandates take interest and enter the story; for example: moving from a micro-cap < 100 million to small cap 100-500 million is a material lift . If the stock maintains its growth it will likely attract the large cap fund managers and will move into the 500 million to 1 billion and above market cap range. Moving through these market cap hurdles can be very difficult, so I often sell or at least trim the stock after a good run just short of that market cap resistance hurdle. In summary, I like to hold my stocks and let them mature but if the tape turns and I am seeing some red flags show up I will relentlessly sell and move on.

TRADE STRATEGY:

For most small cap stocks this is the most common approach, basically buying the stock in your account and holding it until you sell with the expectation the stock will go up in value. The investor will use the cash on hand in the account on an unleveraged basis. The risk of the trade is limited to how much you have in the trade only.

A leveraged long buy trade has considerably more risk and potentially more return if the trade goes your way. The investor is putting up some of their own capital (margin) and borrowing additional funds from a lender to purchase the stock. The investor creates a tax deduction on some of the lending charges and is buying a stock with the expectation of it going up in value over the long term. The risk is accentuated if the stock price moves against you. You not only lose your original capital but now you also have a margin call and an expectation to immediately pay back part or all of the loaned money. I never recommend leveraged strategies for small cap stocks unless the investor has more than enough capital to cover any margin call and could afford to lose all the initial capital as well as the borrowed funds without any material impact to their lifestyle.

Generally I do not recommend short selling strategies especially with small cap stocks, however in cases where sophisticated investors are very confident a stock will decline in price a short sell may be warranted.

When you short a stock the expectation is the stock price will decline and you will capture a profit.

Short selling a stock has considerable more risk even than leveraged strategies. When you short a stock you are essentially borrowing a stock from another investor and selling it into the market placing the funds into your account. At some point in time when you close your position you take the funds out of your account and buy the stock back and replace it into the clients account.

Below is a simplified version of how a short sell works:

Canada Energy Co. (XCM)

Bob short sell XCM trading at $1.00.

Bob elects to sell short 1,000 shares. He calls the broker. Bob does not own the stock so he must borrow it from the brokerage firm, and they sell the stock into the market at $1.00 x 1,000 = $1,000 is placed in Bob's account.

A week later after the stock has been hit by bad news and is trading at 10 cents Bob closes the position.

Bob buy 1,000 shares of XCM at 10 cents and places them back into the account and the difference is his profit.

1,000 x 0.10= $100

$1,000 -100= $900 profit.

WHAT IF THE TRADE GOES AGAINST BOB AND THE STOCK GOES UP, GETTING CAUGHT IN A SHORT SQUEEZE?

$1,000 in your account after a short sale

XCM is halted pending news. When the market reopens the stock goes up and begins to rise further on unexpectedly great news to $1.90per share. There is now big demand for the stock and knowing there were a number of short positions in the market, no one is selling right away, not even at $1.90. Bob could not buy and close his short even if he wanted to at that price. Bob is forced to bid the stock to $2.00 and close the position (a short squeeze).

1,000 x $2.00 = $2,000 cost to replace the stock less $1,000 off the short sale = $1,000 loss! Bob should consider himself lucky. What if the stock kept rising and Bob could not close the position in time to save himself? Short selling is leverage in reverse (on steroids) so I recommend against it. There are significant profits to be made trading small cap stocks using conservative non leveraged approaches.

PRE TRADE PORTFOLIO RISK CALCULATIONS:

Before calling your broker or signing on to your account to make a trade, make these calculations to ensure you're not betting too much on any 1 trade and keeping all your decisions in the context of the overall wealth plan.

Remember the goal here is total risk adjusted return net of fees and taxes, so you must be aware of how fees and tax choices play into your portfolio decisions.

Price of stock x # of shares = total cost to purchase _____

Commission charges on trade _____

Margin cost associated with trade _____

What % of the total & speculative portfolio is this trade _____

No more that 30% of the total wealth portfolio should be in small cap stocks, and no more that 5% of the total portfolio should ever be in 1 stock.

For example: $100,000 portfolio x 30% = $30,000 to the small cap portion of the portfolio

$30,000 x 5% = no more than $1,500 toward any individual trade. Also look at the liquidity of the stock to ensure you do not hold more than you can sell on normal weekly volume.

For example: if you own 15,000 shares of a certain stock and it only trades 14,000, shares week, you would trim the position by 1,000 shares.

BREAK EVEN TARGET PRICE WITH ALL COMMISSIONS AND FEES INCLUDED:

Stop Loss Rule:

Small cap stocks can be very volatile, so when the market moves against you, learn to react quickly and consider selling a stock to maintain profitability in the overall portfolio.

A stop loss is a predetermined price at which you will exit the stock regardless of what is happening with the story. Your broker can have this number placed on the system so that if the price gets hit the stop is triggered and the stock is sold.

Having a stop loss price is imperative, however I do not favour having these automatically triggered. a I prefer to monitor my positions and place sell orders as per my guidelines.

Price declines of > 5% we will watch closely especially if we see increasing above normal weekly volume. Declining price movements above 10% with any material volume will cause us to re-examine our position. Price drops of 15-25% will almost always cause us to sell off the position in whole or in part. Our goal is always to cut losers quickly and let winners run, so if were hanging on to losing stories were doing the wrong thing. As the well-known trader Dennis Gartman says, do more of what is working and less of what is not.

Understand that small cap stocks will have much higher volatility to them than large cap stocks. So moves of 5-10% can be very normal for smaller issuers. One has to look at the normal trading ranges to get a feel for the individual stock. Once you have a feel for what the normal ranges are then look for trading outside the range. Moves greater than 15-20% to the downside are warning signs to exiting from the stock.

Gut Instincts: *Use your head but trust your gut*

I never ignore my gut instincts and when I do I am usually wrong If your gut is telling you to exit, in the absence of overwhelming evidence, exit.

Be aware of those nasty behavioral biases!. I have always been pretty good at buying and it's the not selling when something was wrong that has caught me. I look for what's wrong, and hunt for cockroaches continuously. Charting your observations on a trade is critical, it gives you a great frame of reference to look back on and learn.

What I learned from the trade:

This is pretty self-explanatory but a material area in my mind. It is an extension of the gut instincts section. We learn best from doing, but also honestly reflecting back on what went well on a trade and what we could have done better. Self-reflection helps us avoid future mistakes.

Notes on the reassessment of a situation: *Has there been any material changes?*

_____
_____
_____
_____

ACTION:

Sell All Position Immediately_____

Sell Partial Position _____

Hold_____ Buy/Add_____

Watch Red Flags closely_____

Watch Green Flags Closely_____

Investing is about opportunity cost. Is there a better investment we should be in or should we stay with what we have? On any position we hold this is a constant weekly activity as well as reviewing the daily trade reviews.

KEY QUESTIONS WE CONSTANTLY ASK OURSELVES:

- What do we own, why do we own it?
- Has anything changed, is there a reason to exit, is there a compelling reason to keep it?
- Is there a better lower risk opportunity?

"DO I NEED TO ACT NOW?"

NON NEGOTIABLE TRADING RULES CHECK LIST:

- Always be a skeptic and ask why this is a good idea, what is my upside potential, what is the downside if it goes wrong?

- Strategic asset allocation and risk tolerance determine size of position ALWAYS. Manage risk with position management.

- My money is my future so stay in the game

- If the reason you entered no longer exists EXIT, EXIT ,EXIT

- Watch and recognize your behavioral bias tendencies, get a sober second thought when required.

- Be merciless on your losers; cut losses quickly; stay within your risk and portfolio limits; watch for red flags always.

- Run winners: be aware of green flags and run the winner until they run out of steam or a red flag appears; never be afraid to take 50 % of the position off the table when you have a healthy profit, let the rest run.

- Ask what my worst case scenario is if I buy this, what can go wrong and if it does, how bad will it be?

- Stay disciplined.

- Ensure due diligence is complete. Is a move in the stock driven by new disruptive technology or driven by a new market/environmental situation? Do not hesitate to think contrarian.

- Never be fooled by the randomness of the market; look for the logic behind a move; if you cannot find rationality to the move it is likely random.

- The market can stay irrational longer than I have money.

- Do not be a pig.

- Do not average down a losing position unless there is absolutely overwhelming evidence you can save the trade.

- Pyramiding, leverage, and using options to advance a winning position should only be used in certain situations and always carefully. Seek exceptional advice if you stray into these risky areas. Generally speaking, long-only small cap trading strategies are sufficient to produce excellent risk adjusted portfolio returns; additional risk is usually not warranted.

RULES ARE MEANT TO BE BROKEN ON OCCASION BUT NOT VERY OFTEN AND ALWAYS WITH GREAT CARE WHEN YOU STRAY.

- 2 Independent Analyst Reports
- Stock Chart
- SEDAR & Edgar bulletins; recent press releases
- Financials MD&A
- TSX Info

APPLYING THE LESSONS LEARNED

- Your money is your future! Act accordingly and stay in the game.
- Let your winners run and ruthlessly sell the losers.
- Take note of key green and red flags during your decision making process, when in doubt think red and play safe.
- Stay disciplined.
- Manage your risk with position size, do not get greedy and become a pig.

Sarah and Garth have been looking at a stock that they identified using the small cap success (www.smallcapsuccess.com) program: Tourmaline Oil Corp (TOU) a TSX listed stock. It has met all the key metrics both technically and fundamentally. It has recently broken through a 50 day moving average to the upside on good volume. Sarah should:

a. Work with Garth, pick a target buy and sell price and execute a buy when the timing is right. Place the stock in the correct account according to position size and risk parameters.

b. Sarah should call Bob for a second opinion from the bowling alley crowd.

c. Sarah should not own any stocks and should stick to gold right now, as it looks like the USA economy is turning downward.

d. Sarah should buy Tourmaline inside and energy ETF, where she could diversify among a number of energy player avoiding single security risk.

e. A & D

Correct answer E: She could choose either, as both may be appropriate depending on her risk tolerance and long term investment objectives.

Chapter #6

Example Scenarios

AND BLANK TRADING TEMPLATES

Now that you are armed with many of the tools you need to be a successful small cap investor it's time to do a little practice. If you are a member of www.smallcapsuccess.com the process will be much easier and quicker for you as we have automated much of the process for you and send you these ideas on a weekly basis.

However whether you are a member or not it is important to understand how we walk through the process to uncover golden opportunities for your portfolio. Anyone can take a name out of the stock pages and quickly and efficiently determine if it is a stock worthy of your time and more importantly your hard earned money.

SCENARIO # 1:

Find the stock pages in your local newspaper; pick a random name or a stock you may be familiar with. Try to identify only those names that would meet the small cap criteria of 100 million to 1 billion market cap.

My habitat is the TSX and TSX-V venture exchange and they are clearly identified in my local paper. I will focus on the TSX-V section.

Step 1: I have located a stock name called Medwell Capital Corp (MWC) that I am curious to look at. As stated in the paper, it is in the top gainers section, had a weekly change of 46.8% to the upside, volume was 559,000 shares traded and closing price was $1.85.

Step 2: Walk through your Tier 1 quick screen, this process should take you approximately 30 minutes, maybe less once you have all the websites identified and you are familiar with where to look for the information. I can usually move through a tier 1 review in about 15 minutes if someone has asked me to look into a stock. Of course this is a fully automated process for members of (www.smallcapsuccess.com) and has been a huge time saver for myself.

TIER 1 PHASE 1 INFO:

Date	Jan 16 2014
Ticker symbol	MWC
Company name	Medwell capital Corp, healthcare focused investment corp.
Industry	Financial
Web address	www.medwellcapital.com
IR contact	1-780-413-7152
Exchange	TSX Venture
Volume / Price behaviour	*Early jan big price spike to downside from $1.85 to $1.26 ; 55,000 shares traded; has clawed back to $1.68*

Daily volumes	1,000 – 2,000
10 day avg volume	5,000
Dividend rate	-
Shares outstanding, FD	7,282,589
Market capitalization	$12.4 million < $500 million small cap threshold
Institutional holdings	>2% & <40%

TIER 1 PHASE 2 INFO:

Current price	$1.68 (<5% change over previous day)
52 week high	$1.95
52 week low	$0.76
50 day average	$1.48
Breakout 9 day past 50	Yes, 2 weeks ago
Breakout 50 past 200	Yes, positive
MacD	0.07

GREEN FLAGS & UPSIDE VOLUME PRICE INCREASING:

- Increased volume and price driven by increasing institutional buying *(check www.stockwatch.com) For example, positive buying by Haywood, a well-known shop with some smart retail brokers and a good institutional desk.*

- Large block trades
- Select institutional buyers
- Positive MACD signs
- Positive press releases

RED FLAGS AND UPSIDE VOLUME PRICE DECLINING:

- Increased Institutional Volume on the sell side

TECHNICAL PATTERNS:

- Reverse Head and Shoulders
- 52 Week high hitting resistance with slowing volume.
- Breakout to the downside, 9 day past the 50 day support line.
- 50 day moving past the 200 day Moving Average.
- Negative MACD Signs,
- Negative Press releases,
- Unexpected CEO/CFO resignations or management: *the big sell order recently requires a look and further investigation*

The stock tilts towards positive Tier 1 indicators and green flags, proceed to a detailed Tier 2 analysis; stock tilts towards negative Tier 1 Indicators and red flags, eliminate

UNDECIDED, MOVE TO WATCH LIST

My recommended Action:_____ (Pass-move on,) although some positive momentum with near term indicators, the

normal weekly volume <10,000 shares (very illiquid). This is also a healthcare investment company, very volatile, speculative, and no dividend stream. Interesting to note on the site that the investment focus is health care but they can also invest elsewhere! This could mean style drift risk down the road.

**No need to even do a Tier 2

SCENARIO #2

Tier 1 Small Cap Quick screen

After reviewing my top prospects list off the (www.smallcapsuccess.com) template I selected Canadian Western Bank as a potential investment opportunity. The key areas I noticed were materially increased volume over the 10 day average and modest price appreciation. The volume number >50% indicated we should take a further look.

TIER 1 PHASE 1 INFO:

Date	Jan 17 2014
Ticker symbol	**CWB**
Company name	*Canadian Western Bank, a regional bank from western Canada, head office in Edmonton Ab, focused on the western Canadian small business segment.*
Industry	Financial
Web address	www.cwbank.com

IR contact	www.investorrelations@cwbank.com
Exchange	TSX
Volume / Price behaviour	*No material volume and price changes; consolidation pattern*
Daily volumes	*798,329*
10 day avg volume	*181,717*
Dividend rate	**19 cents per year**
Shares outstanding, FD	*79,631,406*
Market capitalization	**$2,998 million (large cap)**
Institutional holdings	**>2% & <40%**

TIER 1 PHASE 2 INFO:

Current price	**$38.65** *3 month run has been very strong from $30.00; In September positive 50 200 cross, consolidating, with some short term weakness, but trend line intact.*
52 week high	$38.93
52 week low	$27.50
50 day average	$35.76
Breakout 9 day past 50	Yes, in September
Breakout 50 past 200	Yes, positive
MacD	pos

GREEN FLAGS & UPSIDE VOLUME PRICE INCREASING:

- Increased volume and price driven by increasing institutional buying (large block trades, select institutional buyers check www.stockwatch.com)
- Positive MACD Signs
- Positive Press releases
- *Broad support, material liquidity, short term momentum slowing-consolidating.*

RED FLAGS AND UPSIDE VOLUME PRICE DECLINING:

- Increased Institutional Volume on the sell side

TECHNICAL PATTERNS:

- Reverse Head and Shoulders
- 52 Week high hitting resistance with slowing volume.
- Breakout to the downside, 9 day past the 50 day support line.
- 50 day moving past 200 day Moving Average.
- Negative MACD Signs,
- Negative Press releases,
- Unexpected CEO/CFO resignations or management

POST TIER 1 ANALYSIS:

The stock tilts towards Positive Tier 1 indicators and green flags proceed to a detailed Tier 2 analysis: *Tier 2 warranted, proceed.*

Stock tilts towards Negative Tier 1 Indicators and red flags eliminate; undecided, move to Watch List.

TIER 2 SMALL CAP STOCK GARP ANALYSIS

Date	Jan 17 2014
Company	*Canadian Western Bank, a regional bank from western Canada, head office in Edmonton Ab, focused on the western Canadian small business segment.*
Ticker	CWB
Web Address	www.cwbank.com
Idea Generation Source	Example: www.smallcapsuccess.com
Investor Relations Contact and Number	www.investorrelations@cwbank.com
Market	Banking
Market Cap	$2,998 million

High Quality Dividend equity or Speculation?	High Quality Dividend
# Shares Outstanding Fully Diluted	Financial website/ SEDAR – Corp Filings
Float	
Insider Ownership %	SEDI, SEDAR, www.Canadianinsider.com
1 year, 3 month, 1 week Chart Trend	www.stockcharts.com; TMX.com
Institutional Ownership	www.morningstar.ca; 36.90%; Mawer 4%
News Reports, Bulletins, Press releases	

MACRO ECONOMICS:

Sector	Strong, but dependant on AB economy
Sector Performance and Outlook	3-6-12 months; Neutral
Inflation Trend	Low
Interest Rate Trend	Low

ANALYST RATINGS & FORECASTS

Sentiment Index	*Example: 5 buys, 3 holds, no sells*
Fundamentals	
Earnings Growth	Strong trend
Earnings per Share	2.35
PEG Ratio	2.28
PE Ratio	16.1
Sales Growth	8%
Margins & Trend	Margins increasing
Earnings Forecast Trend	Increasing
Earnings surprise History	2013 year end
Debt to Equity	0.63
Cash on the Balance Sheet	$339 million
Free Cash Flow	After capital expenditures; > $0
Earnings Drivers Rational	Alberta economy; Canadian economy
Current Price	$38.65
12 month Target Price	$41.00
Competitive analysis	Direct competition: Pacific Western, ATB
Business Plan	Solid plan and strategy
Management team, Key Executives	Strong
Quality of Board of Directors	Strong

Strategic Partners and Strong Contracts

Key Questions to ask Management on a conference call or IR-financial analyst:

How did the company make money last year? *Banking, trust, insurance, wealth management*

How did it Make money last quarter? *Lending book of $15 billion*

Are these high or low quality earnings? *high, diverse book, 7 sectors: 35% B.C. ,42% Alberta,7% Saskatchewan,2% Manitoba,14% Ontario- Growth expected outside of Alberta of $1.9 billion investment and growing, No branch voicemail (phone calls only go to people, during business hours); customer service oriented.*

What forces tend to move the sector? *Broad economy in Canada and United States driving energy; They are diversifying theor loan book. Also positive to note that the production based loans < $300 million*

How has the stock performed? Last year; last 3 months; last month, last week, TREND *Trend is very positive with growth of 14% year over year; consolidating and some profit taking.*

Peer comparisons. Who is a threat? *National Bank, ATB Financial, Credit unions.*

What are the comparable PE and PEG ratios? Is it expensive or cheap relative to competitors? *PE Ratio is expensive at 16.1: PEG Ratio is moderate to low.*

How much debt do they carry? How long can they survive (Burn Rate)? *No material debt to be concerned about*

How much debt is due this year? *None; Loan Loss provision is low*

How much Free Cash Flow should it have according to the analyst report? *Dividend payout of 25-30% is expected*

Will they generate enough cash to pay its debts? Will they have to raise more money and dilute shareholders? By how much? *Not a concern*

Can it pay its Debt Next year? *Yes*

Will it have to sell assets to pay its debt? *No*

Make note of Investor Relations comments. (Conference calls)

DETAILED GREEN FLAGS VIEW:

- Increasing Sales Growth (1 point);
- Increasing Earnings Trends (2 points);
- Increasing Margins (1 point);
- Ascending chart trend (2 points);
- Increased volume and price driven by increasing institutional buying (2 points);
- Breakout to the upside 9 day past 50 day; Moving Average 50 past 200 MA (3 points);
- Positive Volume and Price Spike with a 50 day MA cross (3 points);

- Positive 200 Day Moving Average (2 points);
- Positive MACD Signs (1 point);
- Positive Press releases (1 point);
- Consensus earnings forecast positive (1 point);
- Positive analyst sentiment (1 Point);

*Total score and comments:*_____ 10 positive outlook

_____
_____
_____
_____

DETAILED RED FLAGS VIEW:

Critical get out or avoid: (***)

***CEO lying to investors

*** Restated earnings

***Large unexpected selling forcing a Gap down, and blowing through a 50 or 200 day MA support level.

*** Unexpected or unexplained material selling by Key officers and directors

- Negative Regulatory Filings TSX, ASC, SEDAR, EGDAR (-4 points);
- Slowing Sales Growth (-1 point);
- Increasing Inventories (-1 point);
- Unexpected Capital Expenditures (-1 point);

- Shrinking Margins (-2 points);

- Insider Trading (-5 points);

- Excessive Short Positions (-2 points);

- Increased Institutional Volume on the sell side (-3 points);

- Negative Press releases (-3 points);

- Unexpected CEO/CFO resignations or management Changes (-6 points);

- Continuous officers and directors selling down the stock (-4 points);

TECHNICAL PATTERNS:

- Descending chart trend (-3 points);

- Reverse Head and Shoulders (-3 points);

- 52 Week high hitting resistance with slowing volume (-2 points);

- Breakout to the downside past the 50 day support line and 200 day Moving Average (-5 points);

- Negative MACD Signs (-3 points);

Total score and comments: -3 consolidation pattern, *General Economy and loan book related risk, buy on dips tilts positive, but PR high, growth rate positive as it diversifies out of Alberta, this is Canadian economy risk.*

_____
_____
_____

SMALL CAP MILLIONAIRE

TRADING PLAN:

Current Price __38.07__ **12 Month Target** __41.00__

Hold Period Trading Timeline 2 yr >Rational: *This is a good long term growth story ,but slow and steady buy on further weakness, small addition to financial services component of portfolio,37.00 or less with positive trend.*

Trade Strategy:

Watch list __X__

Long _____

Short _____

Risk Reward: _____

Win Probability: _____

Trade Risk Limit: _____

Account Risk Limit: _____

Risk: Calculations:

Price of Stock X # of Shares = total Cost _____

Commission on Trade = _____

Margin Cost = _____

% of Total Portfolio= _____

% of Speculative Portfolio _____

Break Even Target Price _____

Stop Loss Rule _____

BUY & Sell Parametres

_____
_____

GUT INSTINCTS:

_____
_____
_____
_____
_____
_____
_____

ACTION:

Sell All Position Immediately_____

Sell Partial Position _____

Hold_____ **Add**_____

Watch Red Flags closely_____

Watch Green Flags Closely_____

NON NEGOTIABLE TRADING RULES CHECK LIST:

- Always be a skeptic and ask why this is a good idea, what is my upside potential, what is the downside if it goes wrong.

- Strategic asset allocation and risk tolerance determine size of position ALWAYS. Manage risk with Position Management.

- My money is my future so stay in the game.

- If the reason you entered no longer exists EXIT, EXIT, EXIT.

- Watch and recognize your behavioral bias tendencies, get a sober second thought when required.

- Be merciless on your losers, cut losses quickly and stay within your risk and portfolio limits. Watch for red flags always.

- Run winners. Be aware of green flags and run the winner until they run out of steam or a red flag appears. Never be afraid to take 50 % of the position off the table when you have a healthy profit and let the rest run.

- Ask what my worst case scenario is if I buy this. Stay disciplined.

- Is a move in the stock driven by new disruptive technology or driven by a new market/environmental situation? Ensure due diligence is complete.

- Do not hesitate to think contrarian.

- Never be fooled by the randomness of the market; look for the logic behind a move; if you cannot find rationality to the move it is likely random.

- The market can stay irrational longer than I have money.

- Do not be a pig.

- Do Not average down a losing position unless there is absolutely overwhelming evidence you can save the trade.

- Pyramiding, leverage, and using options to advance a winning position should only be used in certain situations and always carefully. Seek exceptional advice if you stray into these risky areas. Generally speaking long only small cap trading strategies are sufficient to produce excellent risk adjusted portfolio returns; additional risk is usually not warranted.

- Rules are meant to be broken on occasion but not very often and always with great care when you stray.

FINAL REVIEW CHECK LISTS:

- 2 Independent Analyst Reports
- Stock Chart
- SEDAR & Edgar Bulletins recent press releases
- Financials MD&A
- TSX Info

Chapter #7

My Final Thoughts

So there we have it, you now posses a comprehensive roadmap to help you achieve financial freedom by trading small cap stocks. As you can see there is no free lunch, you have to do the work to arrive at the correct conclusion. However if you follow the rules with some degree of discipline you should be able to navigate the shark infested small cap waters.

IN SUMMARY THERE ARE 5 KEY ELEMENTS TO THIS PLAN:

1. Start with the end goal in mind; like Sarah seek great financial planning advice and begin with an asset allocation and approach that helps you achieve your long term goals and minimizes your risk. Add small cap stocks where appropriate, and follow the fundamental rules we have laid out in the book.

2. Find the right small cap stocks. Note that most will not make the cut, so be selective. You're looking for the real gems; learn how to make your life easier and your selection process more efficient by becoming a member of www.smallcapsuccess.com.

3. Analyze the stocks with an appropriate level of due diligence. Do not be afraid to ask questions and always be skeptical, turn over every rock you can and when you see a cockroach, always assume there are more and avoid the stock.

4. Buy when the odds/green flags are in your favour, be patient and let your winners run, prudently take profits and avoid becoming a pig. Do your own homework; never act on tips from friends, brokers and promoters without taking all the due diligence precautions the book recommends. Do not be like Bob: remember your friends tip is likely their liquidity event and you are the next sucker in line.

5. Ruthlessly sell when the conditions under which you first bought tell you to sell. Identifying your behavioral blind spots is key to any success you will have. Drop the ego; focus on the rules that will drive your success. Selling is what separates the focussed investor from the amateur in this game. Never be afraid to take a profit or exit a losing position that has fundamentally turned. Winning is a game of probabilities, cut the losers and run with the winners.

Enjoy and share the spoils of your success, life is short
Good luck and God Bless

Bill Ross

Biography:

BILL ROSS BHSC, CIM, CFP

Following a 20 year career in the financial services industry as an Investment advisor, manager, and wealth specialist. Bill remains an active investor, entrepreneur and lecturer. Bill resides in Calgary, Alberta Canada with his wife Sheila and his two children Nick and Sarah.

Bill is the CEO of LH Opportunities Group Inc., and is the owner - managing director for the website and investment newsletter, (www.smallcapsucccess.com).

SMALL CAP SUCCESS
Ordinary People Earning Extraordinary Profits

Testimonials

A great read ,a very solid systematic approach to trading stocks.

Tim Conn
President Tatum Corp

One of the best small cap investing books I have read, a real gem for those looking to win trading small cap stocks.

Mollick Hussain, CFA MBA
Corporate Finance Department Enbridge

Printed in Canada